PENGUIN BOOKS

SHOP CLASS AS SOULCRAFT

Matthew B. Crawford is a philosopher and mechanic. He has a Ph.D. in political philosophy from the University of Chicago and served as a postdoctoral fellow on its Committee on Social Thought. Currently a fellow at the Institute for Advanced Studies in Culture at the University of Virginia, he owns and operates Shockoe Moto, an independent motorcycle repair shop in Richmond, Virginia.

Praise for *Shop Class as Soulcraft*

Christian Science Monitor's Best of 2009
San Francisco Chronicle's Best Books of 2009
New York Times Notable Books
Publishers Weekly Best Books of 2009

"An unusual and compelling book that seduces us to succumb to the passions that are dormant within us, begging for release."
—*San Francisco Chronicle*

"A powerful case for the special value of skilled work that requires the use of one's hands." —*The Wall Street Journal*

"*Shop Class as Soulcraft* is a beautiful little book about human excellence and the way it is undervalued in contemporary America."
—Francis Fukuyama, *The New York Times Book Review*

"The sleeper hit of the publishing season. . . . The book makes a persuasive case that knowing how to build and fix things—from framing a house to repairing a leaky toilet—is often far more rewarding than becoming another 'knowledge worker' with no practical skills."
—*The Boston Globe*

"Crawford's book arrives just as a vague sense of dissatisfaction with the demands and rewards of the modern economy is coalescing into something like a movement. . . . Crawford wants his readers to become better, happier, more productive workers. Who could argue with that?" —*The New Yorker*

"[*Shop Class as Soulcraft* is] the one that may upend your preconceptions about labor and, just maybe, cause you to rethink your career (or how you spend your weekends). . . . The book is both impassioned and profound."   —Christopher Shea, *The Washington Post*

"[Crawford] packs plenty of intellectual firepower into his polemic, quoting Aristotle in his own translation and sprinkling the text with erudite footnotes. Like Robert M. Pirsig's *Zen and the Art of Motorcycle Maintenance*, Crawford's book reveals both why we do what we do and why the way we do it is important."   —*Time*

"[Crawford] is onto something big in *Shop Class*, something about how the national culture has gotten so disdainful of physical labor that it is losing some basic precepts of how to live a contented (and competent) life."   —*The Washington Post*

"Spine-tingling." —*New York Magazine*
(approval matrix: "brilliant" and "highbrow")

"Crawford's wry, unaffected voice, humility and clarity [make] *Shop Class* a latter day *Zen*. Like Pirsig, Crawford doesn't talk about philosophy like someone standing at a podium in tweed."
—*Chicago Tribune*

"With so many boom-time values dying along with millions of jobs, [*Shop Class as Soulcraft*] may have arrived at just the right moment."
—*Newsweek*

"Its thought-provoking themes are well worth considering . . . as millions of unemployed Americans struggle to find work, any kind of work, let alone work that suits their skills and talents and offers, in Crawford's words, 'a tighter connection between life and livelihood.'"
—*The Philadelphia Inquirer*

"*Shop Class as Soulcraft* plumbs the logic of the modern economy and examines the fundamental role of labor in it. . . . Crawford takes readers on a romp through the seamy warehouse that houses his Richmond, Virginia, motorcycle repair shop, and he draws upon the writings of Aristotle and Tocqueville to understand what it is that makes work worthwhile. . . . [Crawford] offers us a philosophy of work, and his personal testimony will resonate with many readers. It may cause some to rethink what they do for a living." —*The Washington Times*

"Crawford's writing is remarkably clear and close to the bone. . . . Recent press coverage has sent word-of-mouth buzz on *Shop Class* through the roof, but it really is a book whose time, in our culture, has come." —Susan Salter Reynolds, *Los Angeles Times*

"Crawford makes a philosophical case for choosing the trades over college in his brilliant new book, *Shop Class as Soulcraft*, which launches an intellectually formidable attack on the way our culture has come to devalue manual labor. This bracingly countercultural book, written by a scholar who left white-collar work to open a motorcycle repair shop, defiantly rejects received wisdom about the meaning of work in America today." —*The Dallas Morning News*

"A powerful case for the rewards of manual work." —Matthew Battles, *The Christian Science Monitor*

"Just three days after publication, *Shop Class* reached number 23 on *The New York Times* bestseller list. And in the following three weeks, it went through five printings. When *The New York Times Magazine* ran a 5,000-word excerpt, readers responded on the newspaper's Web site with comments like: 'Without doubt the best article that I have read in 13 years. Thank-you'; 'This is a wonderful, thought-provoking piece. I read it with mixed emotions: elation, admiration, envy, empathy, inadequacy'; and 'You have no idea how much this article means to me. I suspect—hope—it represents the beginning of a shift in thinking.' Americans, perhaps, have found their guide." —*Financial Times*

"Crawford has been able to reach that rare balance between thinking and doing. His new book, *Shop Class as Soulcraft*, shows the rest of us how we can achieve the same equilibrium. . . . Highly readable . . . worth reading . . . Philosophers, mechanics, and anyone who needs to work in this life will be wise to listen to his advice." —*Richmond Times Dispatch*

Shop Class
as Soulcraft

An Inquiry into the Value of Work

Matthew B. Crawford

Penguin Books

PENGUIN BOOKS

Published by the Penguin Group

Penguin Group (USA) Inc., 375 Hudson Street, New York, New York 10014, U.S.A. •
Penguin Group (Canada), 90 Eglinton Avenue East, Suite 700, Toronto, Ontario,
Canada M4P 2Y3 (a division of Pearson Penguin Canada Inc.) • Penguin Books Ltd, 80 Strand,
London WC2R 0RL, England • Penguin Ireland, 25 St Stephen's Green, Dublin 2, Ireland
(a division of Penguin Books Ltd) • Penguin Group (Australia), 250 Camberwell Road,
Camberwell, Victoria 3124, Australia (a division of Pearson Australia Group Pty Ltd) •
Penguin Books India Pvt Ltd, 11 Community Centre, Panchsheel Park,
New Delhi – 110 017, India • Penguin Group (NZ), 67 Apollo Drive, Rosedale,
North Shore 0632, New Zealand (a division of Pearson New Zealand Ltd) •
Penguin Books (South Africa) (Pty) Ltd, 24 Sturdee Avenue,
Rosebank, Johannesburg 2196, South Africa

Penguin Books Ltd, Registered Offices:
80 Strand, London WC2R 0RL, England

First published in the United States of America by The Penguin Press,
a member of Penguin Group (USA) Inc. 2009
Published in Penguin Books 2010

1   3   5   7   9   10   8   6   4   2

Copyright © Matthew B. Crawford, 2009
All rights reserved

Line drawings by Thomas van Auken

THE LIBRARY OF CONGRESS HAS CATALOGED
THE HARDCOVER EDITION AS FOLLOWS:
Crawford, Matthew B.
Shop class as soulcraft : an inquiry into the value of work / by Matthew B. Crawford.
p.   cm.
Includes bibliographical references.
ISBN 978-1-59420-223-0 (hc.)
ISBN 978-0-14-311746-9 (pbk.)
1. Work.   I. Title.
HD4824.C72   2009
331—dc22

Printed in the United States of America
Designed by Michelle McMillian

For my girls,
the whole happy troupe
B, G & J

And in loving memory of my father,
Frank S. Crawford, Jr.

Contents

Introduction

nyone looking for a good used machine tool should talk to Noel Dempsey, a dealer in Richmond, Virginia. Noel's bustling warehouse is full of metal lathes, milling machines, and table saws, and it turns out that much of it once resided in schools. EBay is awash in such equipment, also from schools. Most of this stuff has been kicking around the secondhand market for about fifteen years; it was in the 1990s that shop class started to become a thing of the past, as educators prepared students to become "knowledge workers."

The disappearance of tools from our common education is the first step toward a wider ignorance of the world of artifacts we inhabit. And, in fact, an engineering culture has developed in recent years in which the object is to "hide the works," rendering many of the devices we depend on every day unintelligible to direct inspection. Lift the hood on some cars now (especially German ones), and the engine appears a bit like the shimmering, featureless obelisk that so enthralled the proto-humans in the opening scene of the movie *2001: A Space*

Odyssey. Essentially, there is another hood under the hood. This creeping concealedness takes various forms. The fasteners holding small appliances together now often require esoteric screwdrivers not commonly available, apparently to prevent the curious or the angry from interrogating the innards. By way of contrast, older readers will recall that until recent decades, Sears catalogues included blown-up parts diagrams and conceptual schematics for all appliances and many other mechanical goods. It was simply taken for granted that such information would be demanded by the consumer.

A decline in tool use would seem to betoken a shift in our relationship to our own stuff: more passive and more dependent. And indeed, there are fewer occasions for the kind of spiritedness that is called forth when we take things in hand for ourselves, whether to fix them or to make them. What ordinary people once made, they buy; and what they once fixed for themselves, they replace entirely or hire an expert to repair, whose expert fix often involves replacing an entire system because some minute component has failed.

In this book I would like to speak up for an ideal that is timeless but finds little accommodation today: manual competence, and the stance it entails toward the built, material world. Neither as workers nor as consumers are we much called upon to exercise such competence, most of us anyway, and merely to recommend its cultivation is to risk the scorn of those who take themselves to be the most hardheaded: the hardheaded economist will point out the "opportunity costs" of spending one's time making what can be bought, and the hardheaded educator will say that it is irresponsible to educate the young for the trades, which are somehow identified as jobs of the past. But we might pause to consider just how hardheaded these presumptions are, and whether they don't, on the contrary, issue from a peculiar sort of idealism, one that insistently steers young people toward the most ghostly kinds of work.

Around 1985, articles began to appear in education journals with such titles as "The Soaring Technology Revolution" and "Preparing Kids for High-Tech and the Global Future." Of course, there is nothing new about American futurism. What is new is the wedding of futurism to what might be called "virtualism": a vision of the future in which we somehow take leave of material reality and glide about in a pure information economy. New and yet not so new—for fifty years now we've been assured that we are headed for a "postindustrial society." While manufacturing jobs have certainly left our shores to a disturbing degree, the manual trades have not. If you need a deck built, or your car fixed, the Chinese are of no help. Because they are in China. And in fact there are chronic labor shortages in both construction and auto repair. Yet the trades and manufacturing have long been lumped together in the mind of the pundit class as "blue collar," and their requiem is intoned. More recently, this consensus has begun to show signs of cracking; in 2006 the *Wall Street Journal* wondered whether "skilled [manual] labor is becoming one of the few sure paths to a good living."

This book is concerned less with economics than it is with the *experience* of making things and fixing things. I also want to consider what is at stake when such experiences recede from our common life. How does this affect the prospects for full human flourishing? Does the use of tools answer to some permanent requirement of our nature? Arguing for a renewed cultivation of manual competence puts me at odds with certain nostrums surrounding work and consumption, so this book is in part a cultural polemic. I mean to clarify the origins of, and thereby interrogate, those assumptions that lull us into accepting as inevitable, or even desirable, our increasing manual disengagement.

I will be making frequent reference to my own work experience, most recently as a motorcycle mechanic. Seeing a motorcycle about to leave my shop under its own power, several days after arriving in the back of a pickup truck, I suddenly don't feel tired, even though I've been standing on a concrete floor all day. Through the portal of his helmet, I think I can make out the edges of a grin on the face of a guy who hasn't ridden his bike in a while. I give him a wave. With one of his hands on the throttle and the other on the clutch, I know he can't wave back. But I can hear his salute in the exuberant "bwaaAAAAP! blum-blum" of a crisp throttle, gratuitously revved. That sound pleases me, as I know it does him. It's a ventriloquist conversation in one mechanical voice, and the gist of it is "Yeah!"

The wad of cash in my pants feels different than the checks I cashed in my previous job. Following a doctorate in political philosophy at the University of Chicago, I took a job as executive director of a Washington "think tank." I was always tired, and honestly could not see the rationale for my being paid at all—what tangible goods or useful services was I providing to anyone? This sense of uselessness was dispiriting. The pay was good, but it truly felt like *compensation*, and after five months I quit to open the bike shop. It may be that I am just not well suited to office work. But in this respect I doubt there is anything unusual about me. I offer my own story here not because I think it is extraordinary, but rather because I suspect it is fairly common. I want to do justice to intuitions that many people have, but which enjoy little public credit. This book grows out of an attempt to understand the greater sense of agency and competence I have always felt doing manual work, compared to other jobs that were officially recognized as "knowledge work." Perhaps most surprisingly, I often find manual work more engaging *intellectually*. This book is an attempt to understand why this should be so.

My examples are drawn mostly from the mechanical repair and building trades because that is what I am familiar with (I used to work as an electrician), but I believe the arguments I offer can illuminate other kinds of work as well. It so happens that most of the characters who appear in this book are men, but I am sure that women, no less than men, will recognize the appeal of tangible work that is straightforwardly useful.

Allow me to say a word about what this book is *not*. I want to avoid the kind of mysticism that gets attached to "craftsmanship" while doing justice to the very real satisfactions it offers. I won't be talking about Japanese sword makers or any such thing, and generally prefer to use the term "trade" over "craft" to emphasize the everyday nature of my subject (though I won't observe this distinction rigorously). Compared to any real craftsman, my own skills are execrable, so I have no basis for talking about the higher spirituality that is alleged to arise from a perfectly fit mortise or whatever. As a rough working formula, we might say that craftsmanship, as an ideal, provides the standards, but that in a mass-market economy such as ours, it is the tradesman who exemplifies an economically viable way of life, one that is broadly available and provides many of the same satisfactions we associate with craftsmanship. Also, we tend to think of the craftsman as working in his own snug workshop, while the tradesman has to go out and crawl under people's houses, or up a pole, and make someone else's stuff work. So I want to avoid the precious images of manual work that intellectuals sometimes traffic in. I also have little interest in wistful notions of a "simpler" life that is somehow more authentic, or more democratically valorous for being "working class." I do, in fact, want to rehabilitate the honor of the trades, as being choice-worthy work, but to do so from within my own experience, which I find is not illuminated by any of these fraught cultural ideals. Hardly any of the people I have worked with as an electrician or a mechanic have fit the stock image of "blue collar." Quite a few have been eccentrics—refugees from some more confining life. Some drift in and out of the work, as I have, as their circumstances dictate.

This book advances a nested set of arguments on behalf of work that is meaningful because it is genuinely useful. It also explores what we might call the ethics of maintenance and repair, and in doing so I hope it will speak to those who may be unlikely to go into the trades professionally but strive for some measure of self-reliance—the kind that requires focused engagement with our material things. We now like our things not to disturb us. Why do some of the current Mercedes models have no dipstick, for example? What are the attractions of being disburdened of involvement with our own stuff? This basic question about consumer culture points to some basic questions about work, because in becoming less obtrusive, our devices also become more complicated. How has the relentless complication of cars and motorcycles, for example, altered the jobs of those who service them? We often hear of the need for an "upskilling" of the workforce, to keep up with technological change. I find the more pertinent issue to be: What sort of personality does one need to have, as a twenty-first-century mechanic, to tolerate the layers of electronic bullshit that get piled on top of machines?

What follows is an attempt to map the overlapping territories intimated by the phrases "meaningful work" and "self-reliance." Both ideals are tied to a *struggle for individual agency*, which I find to be at the very center of modern life. When we view our lives through the lens of this struggle, it brings certain experiences into sharper focus. Both as workers and as consumers, we feel we move in channels that have been projected from afar by vast impersonal forces. We worry that we are becoming stupider, and begin to wonder if getting an adequate *grasp* on the world, intellectually, depends on getting a handle on it in some literal and active sense.

Some people respond by learning to grow their own vegetables. There are even reports of people raising chickens on the rooftops of apartment buildings in New York City. These new agrarians say they get a deep satisfaction from recovering a more direct relationship to the food they eat. Others take up knitting, and find pride in wearing clothes they have made themselves. The home economics of our grandmothers is suddenly cutting-edge chic—why should this be?

In hard economic times, we want to be frugal. Frugality requires some measure of self-reliance—the ability to take care of your own stuff. But the new interest in self-reliance seems to have arisen before the specter of hard times. Frugality may be only a thin economic rationalization for a movement that really answers to a deeper need: We want to feel that our world is intelligible, so we can be responsible for it. This seems to require that the provenance of our things be brought closer to home. Many people are trying to recover a field of vision that is basically human in scale, and extricate themselves from dependence on the obscure forces of a global economy.

I would like to consider whether this poignant longing for responsibility that many people experience in their home lives may be (in part) a response to changes in the world of work, where the experience of individual agency has become elusive. Those who work in an office often feel that, despite the proliferation of contrived metrics they must meet, their job lacks objective standards of the sort provided by, for example, a carpenter's level, and that as a result there is something arbitrary in the dispensing of credit and blame. The rise of "teamwork" has made it difficult to trace individual responsi-

bility, and opened the way for new and uncanny modes of manipulation of workers by managers, who now appear in the
guise of therapists or life coaches. Managers themselves inhabit
a bewildering psychic landscape, and are made anxious by the
vague imperatives they must answer to. The college student interviews for a job as a knowledge worker, and finds that the corporate recruiter never asks him about his grades and doesn't
care what he majored in. He senses that what is demanded of
him is not knowledge but rather that he project a certain kind
of personality, an affable complaisance. Is all his hard work in
school somehow just for show—his ticket to a Potemkin meritocracy? There seems to be a mismatch between form and content, and a growing sense that the official story we've been
telling ourselves about work is somehow false.

The time is ripe to dwell on this unease rather than dismiss
it. The scope of the economic crisis is still uncertain as I write
this; it may turn out to be a mere disturbance, soon forgotten.
But, however briefly, we are experiencing a genuine crisis of
confidence in our most prestigious institutions and professions.
This presents an opportunity to reconsider some basic assumptions. The question of what a good job looks like—of
what sort of work is both secure and worthy of being honored—
is more open now than it has been for a long time. Wall
Street in particular has lost its luster as a destination for smart
and ambitious young people. Out of the current confusion of
ideals and confounding of career hopes, a calm recognition may
yet emerge that productive labor is the foundation of all pros-
perity. The meta-work of trafficking in the surplus skimmed
from other people's work suddenly appears as what it is, and it

becomes possible once again to think the thought, "Let me make myself useful."

Back to basics, then. The cover is cracked. It is time to rip it off, look directly at the inner workings, and begin to fix things for ourselves.

1

A Brief Case for the Useful Arts

[I]n schools, we create artificial learning environments for our children that they know to be contrived and undeserving of their full attention and engagement. . . . Without the opportunity to learn through the hands, the world remains abstract, and distant, and the passions for learning will not be engaged.

—DOUG STOWE, WISDOM OF THE HANDS (BLOG), OCTOBER 16, 2006

Tom Hull teaches welding, machine shop, auto shop, sheet metal work, and computer-aided drafting at Marshfield High School in Coos Bay, Oregon. He is also president of the Technology Educators of Oregon. Asked about the current state of his profession, he says a lot of schools shut down their shop class programs in the 1990s, when there was a big push for computer literacy. To pay for the new computers, electives were cut. Shop was especially attractive as a target: it is expensive and potentially dangerous. Further, as Hull says, "you can't shove fifty students at a time into a shop class, like you can a PE class." In California, three-quarters of high school shop programs have disappeared since the early 1980s, according to the California Industrial and Technology Education Association.[1] There are efforts in North Carolina, Florida, and California to revive shop, but finding people competent to teach it has become difficult. "We have a generation of students that can answer questions on standardized tests, know factoids, but they can't do anything," according to Jim Aschwanden, executive director of the California Agricultural Teachers' Association.[2]

Meanwhile, people in the trades are constantly howling about their inability to find workers. The slack has been taken up to some extent by community colleges that offer shop class. Tom Thompson, of Oregon's Department of Education, says there is anecdotal evidence to suggest that one of the fastest-growing segments of the student body at community colleges is people who already have a four-year degree and return to get a marketable trade skill. There are also for-profit schools such as Universal Technical Institute and Wyoming Technical Institute that draw students from around the country. Both graduate about 95 percent of their students, and about 98 percent of those who graduate get jobs in their first year after finishing.

Hull sends out a quarterly newsletter to the graduates of his shop programs. It is like a nineteenth-century almanac, a combination of useful information and intellectual inquiry, as well as examples of human uplift. The newsletter includes shop tips (for example, clever ways to clamp an irregularly shaped object in preparation for welding), book reviews, digressions on aesthetics, and success stories in which he profiles the careers of his former students. A recent issue featured Kyle Cox, a welder and fabricator for Tarheel Aluminum. Hull caught up with his former student as he fabricated an all-aluminum pile-driving barge on the docks in Charleston. Cox says the job changes every day, and that's what he loves about it. He also likes being "useful to the world."

One of Hull's recent columns reflected on the Fibonacci sequence, an infinite series of numbers where the ratio between adjacent pairs approaches a certain value known as the golden ratio, found throughout nature. Hull writes, "the sequence portrays a human characteristic as well, as the ratio is not immediately achieved, but gets closer and closer, and not by some steady slope to perfection but by *self-correcting oscillations*" about the ideal value. This seems to capture the kind of iterated self-criticism, in light of some ideal that is never quite attained, whereby the craftsman advances in his art. You give it your best, learn from your mistakes, and the next time get a little closer to the image you started with in your head. Hull clearly has a humanist's view of what is now called "Career and Technical Education," and plays a major role in the lives of his students. He says his work as a shop teacher is "the best job I can imagine."

Many educators find their work fulfilling. Is there something about the useful arts in particular that can elicit such devotion? For one gets the sense that Hull takes himself to be pointing his students not just to a livelihood but to some more comprehensive view of what a good life looks like.

The Psychic Satisfactions of Manual Work

I started working as an electrician's helper shortly before I turned fourteen. I wasn't attending school at that time and worked full-time until I was fifteen, then kept the trade up during the summers while in high school and college, with steadily increasing responsibility.[3] When I couldn't get a job with my college degree in physics, I was glad to have something to fall back on, and went into business for myself, in Santa Barbara.

I never ceased to take pleasure in the moment, at the end of a job, when I would flip the switch. "And there was light." It was an experience of agency and competence. The effects of my work were visible for all to see, so my competence was real for others as well; it had a social currency. I was sometimes quieted at the sight of a gang of conduit entering a large panel in an industrial setting, bent into nestled, flowing curves, with varying offsets, that somehow all terminated in the same plane. This was a skill so far beyond my abilities that I felt I was in the presence of some genius, and the man who bent that conduit surely imagined this moment of recognition as he worked. As a residential and light-commercial electrician, most of my work got covered up inside walls. Still, I felt pride in meeting the aesthetic demands of a workmanlike installation. Maybe another electrician would see it someday. Even if not, I felt responsible to my better self. Or rather, to the thing itself—craftsmanship has been said to consist simply in the desire to do something well, for its own sake. If the primary satisfaction is intrinsic and private in this way, there is nonetheless a sort of self-disclosing that takes place. As the philosopher Alexandre Kojève writes,

> *The man who works recognizes his own product in the World that has actually been transformed by his work: he recognizes himself in it, he sees in it his own human reality,*

in it he discovers and reveals to others the objective reality
of his humanity, of the originally abstract and purely sub-
jective idea he has of himself.[4]

The satisfactions of manifesting oneself concretely in the world through manual competence have been known to make a man quiet and easy. They seem to relieve him of the felt need to offer chattering *interpretations* of himself to vindicate his worth. He can simply point: the building stands, the car now runs, the lights are on. Boasting is what a boy does, because he has no real effect in the world. But the tradesman must reckon with the infallible judgment of reality, where one's failures or shortcomings cannot be interpreted away. His well-founded pride is far from the gratuitous "self-esteem" that educators would impart to students, as though by magic.

Many people would be reluctant to bestow the term "crafts-manship" on the work of an electrician, and reserve the word for those who make finely wrought objects. This seems a fair reservation, and I see no need to quarrel with it.[5] My own experience in making craft objects is limited to that of a hobbyist, but is perhaps worth relating. People who make their own furniture will tell you that it is hard to justify economically, and yet they persist. Shared memories attach to the material souvenirs of our lives, and producing them is a kind of communion, with others and with the future. I once built a mahogany coffee table on which I spared no expense of effort. At that time I had no immediate prospect of becoming a father, yet

I imagined a child who would form indelible impressions of this table and know that it was his father's work. I imagined the table fading into the background of a future life, the defects in its execution as well as inevitable stains and scars becoming a surface textured enough that memory and sentiment might cling to it, in unnoticed accretions. More fundamentally, as Hannah Arendt writes, the durable objects of use produced by men "give rise to the familiarity of the world, its customs and habits of intercourse between men and things as well as between men and men." "The reality and reliability of the human world rest primarily on the fact that we are surrounded by things more permanent than the activity by which they were produced, and potentially even more permanent than the lives of their authors."[6]

All material things turn to dust, ultimately, so perhaps "permanance" isn't quite the right idea to invoke here. The moral significance of work that grapples with material things may lie in the simple fact that such things lie outside the self. A washing machine, for example, surely exists to serve our needs, but in contending with one that is broken, you have to ask what *it* needs. At such a moment, technology is no longer a means by which our mastery of the world is extended, but an affront to our usual self-absorption. Constantly seeking self-affirmation, the narcissist views everything as an extension of his will, and therefore has only a tenuous grasp on the world of objects as something independent. He is prone to magical thinking and delusions of omnipotence.[7] A repairman, on the other hand, puts himself in the service of others, and fixes the things they depend on. His relationship to objects enacts a more solid sort of command, based on real understanding. For this very reason, his work also chastens the easy fantasy of mastery that permeates modern culture. The repairman has to begin each job by getting outside his own head and noticing things; he has to look carefully and listen to the ailing machine.

The repairman is called in when the smooth operation of our world has been disrupted, and at such moments our dependence on things normally taken for granted (for example, a toilet that flushes) is brought to vivid awareness. The repairman's presence may make the narcissist uncomfortable, then. The problem isn't so much that he is dirty, or uncouth. Rather, he seems to pose a challenge to our self-understanding that is somehow fundamental. We're not as free and independent as we thought. Street-level work that disrupts the infrastructure (the sewer system below or the electrical grid above) brings our *shared* dependence into view. People may inhabit very different worlds even in the same city, according to their wealth or poverty. Yet we all live in the same physical reality, ultimately, and owe a common debt to the world.

Because craftsmanship refers to objective standards that do not issue from the self and its desires, it poses a challenge to the ethic of consumerism, as the sociologist Richard Sennett argued in *The Culture of the New Capitalism*. The craftsman is proud of what he has made, and cherishes it, while the consumer discards things that are perfectly serviceable in his restless pursuit of the new.[8] The craftsman is then more possessive, more tied to what is present, the dead incarnation of past labor; the consumer is more free, more imaginative, and so more valorous according to those who would sell us things. Being able to think materially about material goods, hence critically, gives one some independence from the manipulations of marketing, which as Sennett points out typically divert attention from *what a thing is* to a backstory intimated through associations, the point of which is to exaggerate minor differences between brands. Knowing the production narrative, or at least being able to plausibly imagine it, renders the social narrative of the advertisement less potent. The craftsman has an impoverished fantasy life compared to the ideal consumer; he is more utilitarian and less given to soaring hopes. But he is also more independent.

This would seem to be significant for any political typology. Political theorists from Aristotle to Thomas Jefferson have questioned the republican virtue of the artisan, finding him too narrow in his concerns to be moved by the public good. Yet this assessment was made before the full flowering of mass communication and mass conformity, which pose a different set of problems for the republican character: enervation of judgment and erosion of the independent spirit. If the modern personality is being reorganized on a predicate of passive consumption, this is bound to affect our political culture.

Since the standards of craftsmanship issue from the logic of things rather than the art of persuasion, practiced submission to them perhaps gives the craftsman some psychic ground to stand on against fantastic hopes aroused by demagogues, whether commercial or political. Plato makes a distinction between technical skill and rhetoric on the grounds that rhetoric "has no account to give of the real nature of things, and so cannot tell the cause of any of them."[9] The craftsman's habitual deference is not toward the New, but toward the objective standards of his craft. However narrow in its application, this is a rare appearance in contemporary life—a disinterested, articulable, and publicly affirmable idea of the good. Such a strong ontology is somewhat at odds with the cutting-edge institutions of the new capitalism, and with the educational regime that aims to supply those institutions with suitable workers—pliable generalists unfettered by any single set of skills.

Today, in our schools, the manual trades are given little honor. The egalitarian worry that has always attended tracking students into "college prep" and "vocational ed" is overlaid with another: the fear that acquiring a specific skill set means that one's life is *determined*. In college, by contrast, many students don't learn anything of particular application; college is the ticket to an *open* future. Craftsmanship entails learning to do one thing really well, while the ideal of the new economy is to be able to learn new things, celebrating potential rather than achievement. Somehow, every worker in the cutting-edge workplace is now supposed to act like an "intrapreneur," that is, to be actively involved in the continuous redefinition of his own job. Shop class presents an image of stasis that runs directly counter to what Sennett identifies as "a key element in the new economy's idealized self: the capacity to surrender, to give up possession of an established reality." This stance toward "established reality," which can only be called psychedelic, is best not indulged around a table saw. It is dissatisfied with what Arendt calls the "reality and reliability" of the world. It is a strange sort of ideal, attractive only to a peculiar sort of self—insecurity about the basic character of the world is no fun for most people.

As Sennett argues, most people take pride in being good at something specific, which happens through the accumulation of experience. Yet the flitting disposition is pressed upon workers from above by the current generation of management revolutionaries, for whom the ethic of craftsmanship is actually something to be rooted out from the workforce. Craftsmanship means dwelling on a task for a long time and going deeply into it, because you want to get it right. In managementspeak, this is called being "ingrown." The preferred role model is the management consultant, who swoops in and out and whose very pride lies in his lack of particular expertise. Like the ideal consumer, the management consultant presents an image of soaring freedom, in light of which the manual trades appear cramped and paltry: the plumber with his butt crack, peering under the sink.

With such images in their heads, parents don't want their children to become plumbers. Yet that filthy plumber under the sink might be charging somebody eighty dollars an hour. This fact *ought*, at least, to induce an experience of cognitive dissonance in the parent who regards his child as smart and wants him to become a knowledge worker. If he accepts the basic premise of a knowledge economy that someone being paid a lot of money must *know* something, he may begin to wonder what is really going on under that sink, and entertain a suspicion against the widely accepted dichotomy of knowledge work *versus* manual work. In fact, that dichotomy rests on some fundamental misconceptions. I'd like to offer an alternative account, one that will give due credit to the cognitive richness of the skilled trades. In pursuing these questions, we arrive at insights that help to explain why work that is straightforwardly useful can also be intellectually absorbing.

The Cognitive Demands of Manual Work

In *The Mind at Work,* Mike Rose provides "cognitive biographies" of several trades, and depicts the learning process in a wood shop class. He writes that "our testaments to physical work are so often focused on the values such work exhibits rather than on the thought it requires. It is a subtle but pervasive omission. . . . It is as though in our cultural iconography we are given the muscled arm, sleeve rolled tight against biceps, but no thought bright behind the eye, no image that links hand and brain."[10]

Skilled manual labor entails a systematic encounter with the material world, precisely the kind of encounter that gives rise to natural science. From its earliest practice, craft knowledge has entailed knowledge of the "ways" of one's materials—that is, knowledge of their nature, acquired through disciplined perception. At the beginning of the Western tradition, *sophia* (wisdom) meant "skill" for Homer: the technical skill of a carpenter, for example. Through pragmatic engagement, the carpenter learns the different species of wood, their fitness for such needs as load bearing and water holding, their dimensional stability with changes in the weather, and their varying resistance to rot and insects. The carpenter also gains a knowledge of universals, such as the right angle, the plumb, and the level, which are indispensable for sound construction. It is in the crafts that nature first becomes a thematic object of study, and that study is grounded by a regard for human utility.

In the tradition that developed in the West, "wisdom" lost the concrete sense it originally had in Homer. In religious texts, on the one hand, "wisdom" tended toward the mystical. In science, on the other hand, "wisdom" remained connected to knowledge of nature, but with the advent of idealizations such as the frictionless surface and the perfect vacuum, science, too, adopted a paradoxically otherworldly ideal of *how* we come to know nature: through mental constructions that are more intellectually tractable than material reality, hence amenable to mathematical representation. Descartes, generally credited with inaugurating the scientific revolution, begins from radical doubt about the very existence of an external world, and builds up the principles of scientific inquiry from the foundation of a radically self-contained subject.

Yet this solipsistic ideal doesn't gibe perfectly with the history of science. For in fact, in areas of well-developed craft practices, technological developments typically preceded and gave rise to advances in scientific understanding, not vice versa. The steam engine is a good example. It was developed by mechanics who observed the relations between volume, pressure, and temperature. This was at a time when theoretical scientists were tied to the caloric theory of heat, which later turned out to be a conceptual dead end. The success of the steam engine contributed to the development of what we now call classical thermodynamics. This history provides a nice illustration of a point made by Aristotle:

> *Lack of experience diminishes our power of taking a comprehensive view of the admitted facts. Hence those who dwell in intimate association with nature and its phenomena are more able to lay down principles such as to admit of a wide and coherent development; while those whom devotion to abstract discussions has rendered unobservant of facts are too ready to dogmatize on the basis of a few observations.*[11]

Many inventions capture a reflective moment in which some worker has made explicit the assumptions that are implicit in his skill. In a beautiful article, the cognitive scientists Mike Eisenberg and Ann Nishioka Eisenberg give real pedagogical force to this idea, and draw out its theoretical implications. They offer a computer program to facilitate making origami, or rather Archimedean solids, by unfolding these solids into two dimensions. But they then have their students actually make the solids, out of paper cut according to the computer's instructions. "Computational tools for crafting are entities poised somewhere between the abstract, untouchable world of software objects and the homey constraints of human dexterity; they are therefore creative exercises in making conscious those aspects of craft work . . . that are often more easily represented 'in the hand' than in language."[12] It is worth pausing to consider their efforts, as they have implications well beyond mathematics instruction.

In our early work with HyperGami, we often ran into sit-
uations in which the program provided us with a folding net
that was mathematically correct—i.e., a technically correct
unfolding of the desired solid—but otherwise disastrous. . . .
Here, we are trying to create an approximation to a cone—
a pyramid on a regular octagonal base. HyperGami provides
us with a folding net that will, indeed, produce a pyramid;
but typically, no paper crafter would come up with a net of
this sort, since it is fiendishly hard to join together those
eight tall triangles into a single vertex. In fact, this is an il-
lustrative example of a more general idea—the difficulty of
formalizing, in purely mathematical terms, what it means
to produce a "realistic" (and not merely technically correct)
solution to an algorithmic problem derived from human
practice.

I take their point to be that a realistic solution must include
ad hoc constraints known only through practice, that is,
through embodied manipulations. Those constraints cannot
be arrived at deductively, starting from mathematical entities. These experiments with origami help us to understand
why certain aspects of mechanical work cannot be reduced to
rule following.

When I first starting working in the bike shop, after quitting
the think tank, I would come home from work and my wife
would sniff at me. She'd say "carbs" or "brakes" as she learned
to identify the various solvents used in cleaning different parts

of a motorcycle. Leaving a sensible trace, my workday was at least imaginable to her. But while the filth and odors were apparent, the amount of head scratching I'd done since breakfast was not. Mike Rose writes that in the practice of surgery, "dichotomies such as concrete versus abstract and technique versus reflection break down in practice. The surgeon's judgment is simultaneously technical and deliberative, and that mix is the source of its power."[13] This could be said of any manual skill that is diagnostic, including motorcycle repair. You come up with an imagined train of causes for manifest symptoms and judge their likelihood before tearing anything down. This imagining relies on a stock mental library, not of natural kinds or structures, like that of the surgeon, but rather the functional kinds of an internal combustion engine, their various interpretations by different manufacturers, and their proclivities for failure. You also develop a library of sounds and smells and feels. For example, the backfire of a too-lean fuel mixture is subtly different from an ignition backfire. If the motorcycle is thirty years old, from an obscure maker that went out of business twenty years ago, its proclivities are known mostly through lore. It would probably be impossible to do such work in isolation, without access to a collective historical memory; you have to be embedded in a community of mechanic-antiquarians. These relationships are maintained by telephone, in a network of reciprocal favors that spans the country. My most reliable source, Fred Cousins in Chicago, has such an encyclopedic knowledge of obscure European motorcycles that all I can offer him in exchange is regular deliveries of obscure European beer.

There is always a risk of introducing new complications when working on decrepit machines (kind of like gerontology, I suppose), and this enters the diagnostic logic. Measured in likelihood of screwups, the cost is not identical for all avenues of inquiry when deciding which hypothesis to pursue—for example, when trying to figure out why a bike won't start. The fasteners holding the engine covers on 1970s-era Hondas are Phillips head, and they are usually rounded out and corroded. Do you *really* want to check the condition of the starter clutch, if each of eight screws will need to be drilled out and extracted, risking damage to the engine case? Such impediments can cloud your thinking. Put more neutrally, the attractiveness of any hypothesis is determined in part by physical circumstances that have no logical connection to the diagnostic problem at hand, but a strong pragmatic bearing on it (kind of like origami). The factory service manuals tell you to be systematic in eliminating variables, but they never take into account the risks of working on old machines. So you have to develop your own decision tree for the particular circumstances. The problem is that at each node of this new tree, your own unquantifiable risk aversion introduces ambiguity. There comes a point where you have to step back and get a larger gestalt. Have a cigarette and walk around the lift. Any mechanic will tell you that it is invaluable to have other mechanics around to test your reasoning against, especially if they have a different intellectual disposition.

My shop mate in the early years, Thomas Van Auken, was also an accomplished visual artist (he is the illustrator of this book) and I was repeatedly struck by his ability to literally *see* things that escaped me. I had the conceit of being an empiricist, but seeing things is not always a simple matter. Even on the relatively primitive vintage bikes that were our specialty, some diagnostic situations contain so many variables, and symptoms can be so under-determining of causes, that explicit analytical reasoning comes up short. What is required then is the kind of judgment that arises only from experience; hunches rather than rules. I quickly realized there was more thinking going on in the bike shop than in my previous job at the think tank.

Socially, being the proprietor of a bike shop in a small city gives me a feeling I never had before. I feel I have a place in society. Whereas "think tank" is an answer that, at best, buys you a few seconds when someone asks what you do and you try to figure out what it is that you in fact do, with "motorcycle mechanic" I get immediate recognition. I barter services with machinists and metal fabricators, which has a very different feel than transactions with money, and further increases my sense of belonging to a community. There are three restaurants in Richmond with cooks whose bikes I have restored, where unless I deceive myself I am treated as a sage benefactor. I feel pride before my wife when we go out to dinner and are given preferential treatment, or simply a hearty greeting. There are group rides, and there used to be bike night every Tuesday at a certain bar. Sometimes one or two people would be wearing my shop's T-shirt, which felt good.

Given the intrinsic richness of manual work—cognitively, socially, and in its broader psychic appeal—the question becomes why it has suffered such a devaluation as a component of education. The economic rationale so often offered, namely, that manual work is somehow going to disappear, is question-able if not preposterous, so it is in the murky realm of culture that we must look to understand these things. Here a bit of history can help; a glance at the origins of shop class early in the twentieth century reveals cultural currents that continue to swirl around us.

Art, Crafts, and the Assembly Line

Early in the twentieth century, when Teddy Roosevelt preached the strenuous life and elites worried about their state of "over-civilized" spiritual decay, the project of getting back in touch with "real life" took various forms. One was romantic fantasy about the premodern craftsman. This was understandable given changes in the world of work at the turn of the century, a time when the bureaucratization of economic life was rapidly in-creasing the number of paper shufflers. As T. J. Jackson Lears explains in his history of the Progressive era, *No Place of Grace*, the tangible elements of craft were appealing as an antidote to vague feelings of unreality, diminished autonomy, and a frag-mented sense of self that were especially acute among the pro-fessional classes.

The Arts and Crafts movement thus fit easily with the new therapeutic ethic of self-regeneration. Depleted from his work-week in the corporate world, the office worker repaired to his basement workshop to putter about and tinker, refreshing him-self for the following week. As Lears writes, "toward the end of the nineteenth century, many beneficiaries of modern culture began to feel they were its secret victims."[14] Various forms of antimodernism gained wide currency in the middle and upper classes, including the ethic of craftsmanship. Some Arts and Crafts enthusiasts conceived their task to be evangelizing good taste as embodied in the works of craft, as against machine-age vulgarity. Cultivating an appreciation for objets d'art was thus a form of protest against modernity, with a view to providing a livelihood to dissident craftsmen. But it dovetailed with, and gave a higher urgency to, the nascent culture of luxury consumption. As Lears tells the story, the great irony is that antimodernist sentiments of aesthetic revolt against the machine paved the way for certain unattractive features of late-modern culture: therapeutic self-absorption and the hankering after "authenticity," precisely those psychic hooks now relied upon by advertisers. Such spiritualized, symbolic modes of craft practice and craft consumption represented a kind of compensation for, and therefore an accommodation to, new modes of routinized, bureaucratic work.

But not everyone worked in an office. Indeed, there was class conflict brewing, with unassimilated immigrants accumulating in America's eastern cities and serious labor violence in Chicago and elsewhere. To the upper classes of those same cities, enamored of the craft ideal, the possibility presented itself that the laboring classes might remain satisfied with their material lot if they found joy in their labor. Shop class could serve to put the proper spin on manual work. Any work, it was posited, could be "artful" if done in the proper spirit. Somehow a movement that had started with reverence for the craftsman now offered an apologetic for factory work. As Lears writes,

"By shifting their attention from the conditions of labor to the laborer's frame of mind, craft ideologues could acclaim the value of any work, however monotonous."[15]

The Smith-Hughes Act of 1917 gave federal funding for manual training in two forms: as part of general education and as a separate vocational program. The invention of modern shop class thus serviced both cultural reflexes of the Arts and Crafts movement at once. The children of the managerial class could take shop as enrichment to the college-prep curriculum, making a bird feeder to hang outside Mom's kitchen window, while the children of laborers would be socialized into the work ethic appropriate to their station through what was now called "industrial arts" education. The need for such socialization was not simply a matter of assimilating immigrants from southern and eastern Europe who lacked a Protestant work ethic. It was recognized as a necessity for the broader working-class population, precisely because the institutions that had previously served this socializing function, apprenticeship and guild traditions, had been destroyed by new modes of labor. In his 1915 report to the United States Commission on Industrial Relations, Robert Hoxie worried thus:

> It is evident . . . that the native efficiency of the working class must suffer from the neglect of apprenticeship, if no other means of industrial education is forthcoming. Scientific managers, themselves, have complained bitterly of the poor and lawless material from which they must recruit their workers, compared with the efficient and self-respecting craftsmen who applied for employment twenty years ago.[16]

Needless to say, "scientific managers" were concerned more with the "efficient" part of this formula than with the "self-respecting" part, yet the two are not independent. The quandary was how to make workers efficient and attentive, when their actual labor had been degraded by automation. The motivation previously supplied by the intrinsic satisfactions of manual work was to be replaced with ideology; industrial arts education now concerned itself with moral formation. Lears writes that "American craft publicists, by treating craftsmanship . . . as an agent of socialization, abandoned [the] effort to revive pleasurable labor. Manual training meant specialized assembly line preparation for the lower classes and educational or recreational experiences for the bourgeoisie."[17]

Of the Smith-Hughes Act's two rationales for shop class, vocational and general ed, only the latter emphasized the learning of aesthetic, mathematical, and physical principles through the manipulation of material things. It is not surprising, then, that the act came four years after Henry Ford's innovation of the assembly line. The nascent two-track educational scheme mirrored the assembly line's severing of the cognitive aspects of manual work from its physical execution. Such a partition of thinking from doing has bequeathed us the dichotomy of white collar versus blue collar, corresponding to mental versus manual.

These seem to be the categories that inform the educational landscape even now, and this entails two big errors. First, it assumes that all blue-collar work is as mindless as assembly line work, and second, that white-collar work is still recognizably mental in character. Yet there is evidence to suggest that the new frontier of capitalism lies in doing to office work what was previously done to factory work: draining it of its cognitive elements. Paradoxically, educators who would steer students toward cognitively rich work might do this best by rehabilitating the manual trades, based on a firmer grasp of what such work is really like.

This would take courage. Any high school principal who doesn't claim as his goal "one hundred percent college attendance" is likely to be accused of harboring "low expectations" and run out of town by indignant parents. This indignation is hard to stand against, since it carries all the moral weight of egalitarianism. Yet it is also snobbish, since it evidently regards the trades as something "low." The best sort of democratic education is neither snobbish nor egalitarian. Rather, it accords a place of honor in our common life to whatever is best. At this weird moment of growing passivity and dependence, let us publicly recognize a yeoman aristocracy: those who gain real knowledge of real things, the sort we all depend on every day.

But is it feasible to make a decent living in the trades? Or are we headed for a "postindustrial" society in which there will be little need for the work of the hand? Are we perhaps already there? What are the economics of "the knowledge economy"? My purpose in this book is to elaborate the potential for human flourishing in the manual trades—their rich cognitive challenges and psychic nourishment—rather than stake out policy positions or make factual claims about the economy. But it may be well to consider some economic views that can nourish our skepticism about the postindustrial vision, and open the way for our larger inquiry.

The Future of Work: Back to the Past?

Writing in *Foreign Affairs*, the Princeton economist Alan Blinder considers the question of job security and falling wages for U.S. workers in light of global competition:

> *Many people blithely assume that the critical labor-market distinction is, and will remain, between highly educated (or highly skilled) people and less-educated (or less-skilled) people—doctors versus call-center operators, for example. The supposed remedy for the rich countries, accordingly, is more education and a general "upskilling" of the work force. But this view may be mistaken. . . . The critical divide in the future may instead be between those types of work that are easily deliverable through a wire (or via wireless connections) with little or no diminution in quality and those that are not. And this unconventional divide does not correspond well to traditional distinctions between jobs that require high levels of education and jobs that do not.[18]*

Blinder suggests the crucial distinction in the labor market will be between what he calls "personal services" and "impersonal services." The former either require face-to-face contact or are inherently tied to a specific site. Physicians who treat patients don't need to worry that their jobs will be sent offshore, but radiologists who examine images have already seen this happen, just as accountants and computer programmers have. He goes on to point out that "you can't hammer a nail over the Internet."

Blinder's analysis suggests a future of rising wages for construction, for maintenance and repair work on physical plants, and for maintenance and repair of durable machines (such as cars) that aren't so cheap that they become disposable at the first sign of trouble, as for example a toaster oven is. In a follow-up piece in the *Washington Post*, he writes that "millions of white-collar workers who thought their jobs were immune to foreign competition suddenly find that the game has changed—and not to their liking."[19]

He finds 30 million to 40 million U.S. jobs to be potentially offshorable, ranging from "scientists, mathematicians and editors on the high end" to "telephone operators, clerks and typists on the low end." Blinder predicts a massive economic disruption that is only just beginning, affecting people who went to college and assumed their education prepared them for high-paying careers with lots of opportunity. Now their bosses are looking to India, or the Philippines, and finding well-qualified people who speak good English and will work for a fraction of what Americans have been earning. Architects face this threat, but builders don't.

The MIT economist Frank Levy makes a complementary argument. He puts the issue not in terms of whether a service can be *delivered* electronically or not, but rather whether the service is itself rules-based or not. Until recently, he writes, you could make a decent living doing a job that required you to carefully follow instructions, such as preparing tax returns. But such work is subject to attack on two fronts—some of it goes to off-shore accountants and some of it is done by tax preparation software, such as TurboTax. The result is downward pressure on wages for jobs based on rules.

These economic developments command our attention. The intrusion of computers, and distant foreigners whose work is conceived in a computer-like, rule-bound way, into what was previously the domain of professionals may be alarming, but it also compels us to consider afresh the *human* dimension of work. In what circumstances does the human element remain indispensable, and why? Levy gestures toward an answer when he writes that "viewed from this rules-based perspective, creativity [sic] is knowing what to do when the rules run out or there are no rules in the first place. It is what a good auto mechanic does after his computerized test equipment says the car's transmission is fine but the transmission continues to shift at the wrong engine speed."[20]

When this happens, the mechanic is thrown back on himself and must make sense of the situation. Often this sense making entails not so much problem solving as problem *finding*. When you do the math problems at the back of a chapter in an algebra textbook, you are problem solving. If the chapter is entitled "Systems of two equations with two unknowns," you know exactly which methods to use. In such a constrained situation, the pertinent context in which to view the problem has already been determined, so there is no effort of interpretation required. But in the real world, problems don't present themselves in this predigested way; usually there is too much information, and it is difficult to know what is pertinent and what isn't. Knowing what *kind* of problem you have on hand means knowing what features of the situation can be ignored. Even the boundaries of what counts as "the situation" can be ambiguous; making discriminations of pertinence cannot be achieved by the application of rules, and requires the kind of judgment that comes with experience. The value and job security of the mechanic lie in the fact that he has this firsthand, personal knowledge.

Every trade is different. Each offers its own intrinsic satisfactions, characteristic frustrations, and cognitive challenges; sometimes these challenges are rich enough to be totally absorbing. To understand why the kind of thinking that goes on in the trades isn't more broadly appreciated, let us inquire once more in a historical mode, the better to understand our current situation.

2

The Separation of Thinking from Doing

The dichotomy of mental versus manual didn't arise spontaneously. Rather, the twentieth century saw concerted *efforts* to separate thinking from doing. Those efforts achieved a good deal of success in ordering our economic life, and it is this success that perhaps explains the plausibility the distinction now enjoys. Yet to call this "success" is deeply perverse, for wherever the separation of thinking from doing has been achieved, it has been responsible for the degradation of work. If we can understand the process by which so many jobs get fragmented, we will be better able to recognize those areas of work that have resisted the process, and identify jobs in which the human capacities may be more fully engaged.

In the 1950s, sociologists started pointing out a basic resemblance between Soviet and Western societies: in both there seemed to be an increasing number of jobs that were radically simplified. Both societies were industrial, and had in common a growing separation of planning from execution. This was sometimes attributed to automation, but more penetrating observers noted that it proceeded from the imperatives of rational administration—a sort of social technology, rooted in the division of labor. The "machine" in question was the social body, made up of increasingly standardized parts. In the Soviet bloc, this machine was subject to central control by the state; in the West, by corporations.

In 1974, Harry Braverman published his masterpiece of economic reflection, *Labor and Monopoly Capital: The Degradation of Work in the Twentieth Century.* Braverman was an avowed Marxist. With the cold war now safely decided, we may consider anew, without a sense of mortal political threat, the Marxian account of alienated labor. As Braverman acknowledged, this critique applied to the Soviet Union no less than to capitalist societies. He gives a richly descriptive account of the degradation of many different kinds of work. In doing so, he offers nothing less than an explanation of why we are getting more stupid with every passing year—which is to say, the degradation of work is ultimately a cognitive matter, rooted in the separation of thinking from doing.

The Degradation of Blue-Collar Work

The central culprit in Braverman's account is "scientific management," which "enters the workplace not as the representative of science, but as the representative of management masquerading in the trappings of science."[1] The tenets of scientific management were given their first and frankest articulation by Frederick Winslow Taylor, whose *Principles of Scientific*

Management was hugely influential in the early decades of the twentieth century. Stalin was a big fan, as were the founders of the first MBA program, at Harvard, where Taylor was invited to lecture annually. Taylor writes, "The managers assume . . . the burden of gathering together all of the traditional knowledge which in the past has been possessed by the workmen and then of classifying, tabulating, and reducing this knowledge to rules, laws, and formulae."[2] Scattered craft knowledge is concentrated in the hands of the employer, then doled out again to workers in the form of minute instructions needed to perform some *part* of what is now a work *process*. This process replaces what was previously an integral activity, rooted in craft tradition and experience, animated by the worker's own mental image of, and intention toward, the finished product. Thus, according to Taylor, "All possible brain work should be removed from the shop and centered in the planning or laying-out department. . . ."[3] It is a mistake to suppose that the primary purpose of this partition is to render the work process more efficient. It may or may not result in extracting more value from a given unit of labor *time*. The concern is rather with labor *cost*. Once the cognitive aspects of the job are located in a separate management class, or better yet in a process that, once designed, requires no ongoing judgment or deliberation, skilled workers can be replaced with unskilled workers at a lower rate of pay. Taylor writes that the "full possibilities" of his system "will not have been realized until almost all of the machines in the shop are run by men who are of smaller caliber and attainments, and who are therefore cheaper than those required under the old system."[4]

What becomes of the skilled workers? The naïve view is that "they go elsewhere." But the competitive labor-cost advantage now held by the more modern firm, which has aggressively separated planning from execution, compels the whole industry to follow the same route, and entire skilled trades disappear. Thus craft knowledge dies out, or rather gets instantiated in a different form, as process engineering knowledge. The conception of the work is remote from the worker who does it.

Scientific management introduced the use of "time and motion analysis" to describe the physiological capabilities of the human body in machine terms. As Braverman writes, "the more labor is governed by classified motions which extend across the boundaries of trades and occupations, the more it dissolves its concrete forms into the general types of work motions. This mechanical exercise of human faculties according to motion types which are studied independently of the particular kind of work being done, brings to life the Marxist conception of 'abstract labor.'"[5] The clearest example of abstract labor is thus the assembly line. The *activity* of self-directed labor, conducted by the worker, is dissolved or abstracted into parts and then reconstituted as a *process* controlled by management—a labor sausage.

At the turn of the last century, the manufacture of automobiles was done by craftsmen recruited from bicycle and carriage shops: all-around mechanics who knew what they were doing. In *The Wheelwright's Shop*, George Sturt relates his experience in taking over his family business of making wheels for carriages, in 1884, shortly before the advent of the automobile. He had been a schoolteacher with literary ambitions, but now finds himself almost overwhelmed by the cognitive demands of his new trade. In Sturt's shop, working exclusively with hand tools, the skills required to build a wheel regress all the way to the selection of trees to fell for timber, the proper time for felling them, how to season them, and so forth. To select but one minor task out of the countless he describes, here is Sturt's account of fabricating a section of the wheel's rim, called a "felloe":

> *Yet it is in vain to go into details at this point; for when the simple apparatus had all been gotten together for one simple-looking process, a never-ending series of variations was introduced by the material. What though two felloes might seem much alike when finished? It was the wheelwright himself who had to make them so. He it was who hewed out that resemblance from quite dissimilar blocks, for no two felloe-blocks were ever alike. Knots here, shakes there, rindgalls, waney edges (edges with more or less bark in them), thicknesses, thinnesses, were for ever affording new chances or forbidding previous solutions, whereby a fresh problem confronted the workman's ingenuity every few minutes. He had no band-saw (as now [1923]) to drive, with ruthless unintelligence, through every resistance. The timber was far from being prey, a helpless victim, to a machine. Rather it would lend its own special virtues to the man who knew how to humour it.[6]*

Given their likely acquaintance with such a cognitively rich world of work, it is hardly surprising that when Henry Ford introduced the assembly line in 1913, workers simply walked out. One of Ford's biographers wrote, "So great was labor's distaste for the new machine system that toward the close of 1913 every time the company wanted to add 100 men to its factory personnel, it was necessary to hire 963."[7]

This would seem to be a crucial moment in the history of political economy. Evidently, the new system provoked natural revulsion. Yet, at some point, workers became habituated to it. How did this happen? One might be tempted to inquire in a typological mode: What sort of men were these first, the 100 out of 963 who stuck it out on the new assembly line? Perhaps it was the men who felt less revulsion because they had less pride in their own powers, and were therefore more tractable. Less republican, we might say. But if there was initially such a self-selection process, it quickly gave way to something more systemic.

In a temporary suspension of the Taylorist logic, Ford was forced to double the daily wage of his workers to keep the line staffed. As Braverman writes, this "opened up new possibilities for the intensification of labor within the plants, where workers were now anxious to keep their jobs."[8] These anxious workers were more productive. Indeed, Ford himself later recognized his wage increase as "one of the finest cost-cutting moves we ever made," as he was able to double, and then triple, the rate at which cars were assembled by simply speeding up the conveyors. By doing so he destroyed his competitors, and thereby destroyed the possibility of an alternative way of working. (This also removed the wage pressure that comes from the existence of more enjoyable jobs.) In 1900 there were 7,632 wagon and carriage manufacturers in the United States.[9] Adopting Ford's methods, the industry would soon be reduced to the Big Three. So workers eventually became habituated to the abstraction of the assembly line. Evidently, it inspires revulsion only if one is acquainted with more satisfying modes of work.

Here the concept of wages as *compensation* achieves its fullest meaning, and its central place in modern economy. Changing attitudes toward consumption seemed to play a role. A man whose needs are limited will find the least noxious livelihood and work in a subsistence mode, and indeed the experience of early (eighteenth-century) capitalism, when many producers worked at home on a piece-rate basis, was that only so much labor could be extracted from them. Contradicting the assumptions of "rational behavior," it was found that when employers would increase the piece rate in order to boost production, it actually had the opposite effect: workers would produce less, as now they could meet their fixed needs with less work. Eventually it was learned that the only way to get them to work harder was to play upon the imagination, stimulating new needs and wants. Consumption, no less than production, needed to be brought under scientific management—the management of desire. Thus, there came to be marketers who called themselves "consumption engineers" in the early decades of the twentieth century. They were armed with the latest findings of experimental psychology.[10]

The habituation of workers to the assembly line was thus perhaps made easier by another innovation of the early twentieth century: consumer debt. As Jackson Lears has argued, through the installment plan previously unthinkable acquisitions became thinkable, and more than thinkable: it became normal to carry debt.[11] The display of a new car bought on installment became a sign that one was trustworthy. In a wholesale transformation of the old Puritan moralism, expressed by Benjamin Franklin (admittedly no Puritan) with the motto "Be frugal and free," the early twentieth century saw the moral legitimation of spending. One symptom Lears points to is a 1907 book with the immodest title *The New Basis of Civilization*, by Simon Nelson Patten, in which the moral valence of debt and spending is reversed, and the multiplication of wants becomes not a sign of dangerous corruption but part of the civilizing process. That is, part of the disciplinary process. As Lears writes, "Indebtedness could discipline workers, keeping them at routinized jobs in factories and offices, graying but in harness, meeting payments regularly."

The Degradation of White-Collar Work

Much of the "jobs of the future" rhetoric surrounding the eagerness to end shop class and get every warm body into college, thence into a cubicle, implicitly assumes that we are heading to a postindustrial economy in which everyone will deal only in abstractions. Yet trafficking in abstractions is not the same as thinking. White-collar professions, too, are subject to routinization and degradation, proceeding by the same logic that hit manual fabrication a hundred years ago: the cognitive elements of the job are appropriated from professionals, instantiated in a system or process, and then handed back to a new class of workers—clerks—who replace the professionals. If genuine knowledge work is not growing but actually shrinking, because it is coming to be concentrated in an ever-smaller elite, this has implications for the vocational advice that students ought to receive. If they want to use their brains at work, and aren't destined to make it into the star chamber, they should be helped to find work that somehow thwarts the Taylorist logic, and is therefore safe from it.

It is not always the imperatives of profit that drive the alienation of judgment from professionals; sometimes it is a matter of public policy. Standardized tests remove a teacher's discretion in the curriculum; strict sentencing guidelines prevent a judge from judging. It seems to be our liberal political instincts that push us in this direction of centralizing authority; we distrust authority in the hands of individuals. With its reverence for neutral process, liberalism is, by design, a politics of irresponsibility. This begins with the best of intentions—securing our liberties against the abuse of power—but has become a kind of monster that feeds on individual agency, especially for those who work in the public sector. In the private sector, the monster is created by profit maximization rather than distrust of authority, but it demands a similar diet.

"Expert systems," a term coined by artificial intelligence researchers, were initially developed by the military for battle command, then used to replicate industrial expertise in such fields as oil-well drilling and telephone-line maintenance. Then they found their way into medical diagnosis, and eventually the cognitively murky, highly lucrative regions of financial and legal advice. In *The Electronic Sweatshop: How Computers Are Transforming the Office of the Future into the Factory of the Past*, Barbara Garson details how "extraordinary human ingenuity has been used to eliminate the need for human ingenuity." She finds that, like Taylor's rationalization of the shop floor, the intention of expert systems is "to transfer knowledge, skill, and decision making from employee to employer." While Taylor's time and motion studies broke every concrete work motion into minute parts,

> the modern knowledge engineer performs similar detailed studies, only he anatomizes decision making rather than bricklaying. So the time-and-motion study has become a time-and-thought study. . . . To build an expert system, a living expert is debriefed and then cloned by a knowledge engineer. That is to say, an expert is interviewed, typically for weeks or months. The knowledge engineer watches the expert work on sample problems and asks exactly what factors the expert considered in making his apparently intuitive decisions. Eventually hundreds or thousands of rules of thumb are fed into the computer. The result is a program that can "make decisions" or "draw conclusions" heuristically instead of merely calculating with equations. Like a real expert, a sophisticated expert system should be able to draw inferences from "iffy" or incomplete data that seems to suggest or tends to rule out. In other words it uses (or replaces) judgment.[12]

The human expert who is cloned achieves a vast dominion and immortality, in a sense. It is *other* experts, and future experts, who are displaced as expertise is centralized. "This means that more people in the advice or human service business will be employed as the disseminators, rather than the originators, of this advice," Garson writes. In *The Culture of the New Cap-*

italism, Richard Sennett describes just such a process, "especially in the cutting-edge realms of high finance, advanced technology, and sophisticated services": genuine knowledge work comes to be concentrated in an ever-smaller elite. It seems we must take a cold-eyed view of "knowledge work," and reject the image of a rising sea of pure mentation that lifts all boats. More likely is a rising sea of clerkdom. To expect otherwise is to hope for a reversal in the basic logic of the modern economy—that is, cognitive stratification. It is not clear to me what this hope could be based on, though if history is any guide we have to wonder whether the excitation of such a hope has become an instrument by which young people are prepared for clerkdom, in the same perverse way that the craft ideology prepared workers for the assembly line. Both provide a lens that makes the work look appealing from afar, but only by presenting an image that is upside down.

Everyone an Einstein

The latest version of such hopeful thinking is gathered into the phrase "the creative economy." In *The Rise of the Creative Class*, Richard Florida presents the image of the creative individual. "Bizarre mavericks operating at the bohemian fringe" are now "at the very heart of the process of innovation," forming a core creative class "in science and engineering, architecture and design, education, arts, music, and entertainment," joining "creative professionals in business and finance, law, healthcare and related fields."[13]

In a related article, Florida invokes Albert Einstein to give us some idea of the self-directed and creative individual. This type is becoming more numerous. "Already, more than 40 million Americans work in the creative sector, which has grown by 20 million jobs since the 1980s."[14] Some of these new Einsteins, it turns out, can be found working at Best Buy.

Florida informs us that "Best Buy CEO Brad Anderson has made it his company's stated mission to provide an 'inclusive, innovative work environment designed to unleash the power of all of our people as they have fun while being the best.'" Adopting the role of spokesperson for the spokesperson, Florida continues:

> *Employees are encouraged to improve upon the company's work processes and techniques in order to make the workplace more productive and enjoyable while increasing sales and profits. In many cases, a small change made on the salesroom floor—by a teenage sales rep re-conceiving a Vonage display or an immigrant salesperson acting on a thought to increase outreach, advertising, and service to non-English-speaking communities—has been implemented nationwide, generating hundreds of millions of dollars in added revenue.*

The Vonage display isn't merely altered, it is *re-conceived*. Whatever survives this onslaught of intellectual rigor by the teenage sales rep is put back on the sales floor. Its conceptual foundations clarified, the re-conceived Vonage display generates hundreds of millions of dollars in added revenue. Florida continues:

Best Buy's Anderson . . . likes to say that the great promise of the creative era is that, for the first time in our history, the further development of our economic competitiveness hinges on the fuller development of human creative capabilities. In other words, our economic success increasingly turns on harnessing the creative talents of each and every human being. . . .[15]

Frank Levy, the MIT economist, responds to this by dryly noting that "where I live Best Buy seems to be starting people at about $8.00 an hour."[16]

Florida is unimpressed by such facts. After all, the "stated mission" of Best Buy's CEO is to provide a work environment designed to "unleash the power of all of our people as they have fun while being the best." It seems the unleashed power of all those mavericks in the Best Buy creative sector is fully compatible with near-minimum wage. Bohemians live by a different set of rules; they aren't money-grubbing proles. "They have fun while being the best," these aristocrats of the spirit. Florida presents the image of an immigrant salesperson *acting on a thought.* Are we to believe these teenagers and immigrants working at Best Buy have reclaimed the unity of thought and action of the preindustrial craftsman, or of the gentleman inventor? Florida seems to suggest there has been a wholesale overthrow of the centralization of thinking that is the hallmark of industrial capitalism.

Robert Jackall offers a more plausible account of the role these teenaged and immigrant Einsteins are playing at Best Buy. Based on hundreds of hours of interviews with corporate managers, he concludes that one of the principles of contemporary management is to "push details down and pull credit up."[17] That is, avoid making decisions, because they could damage your career, but then spin cover stories after the fact that interpret positive outcomes to your credit. To this end, upper management deals only with abstractions, not operational details. If things go well: "Finding cross-marketing synergies in the telecommunications and consumer electronics divisions has improved our strategic outlook heading into the fourth quarter." If things go badly: "Change the Vonage display? That was the kid's idea. What's his name, Bapu or something. Jeezus, these immigrants." Where Jackall sees managerial ass covering, Florida sees a magical bubbling up of people power: "harnessing the creative talents of each and every human being."

Florida writes, "the creative content of many working-class and service-class jobs is growing—a prime example being the continuous-improvement programs on many factory floors, which call on line workers to contribute ideas as well as their physical labor."[18] Braverman was familiar with this style of management, characterized by "a studied pretense of worker 'participation,' a gracious liberality in allowing the worker to adjust a machine, replace a light bulb . . . and to have the illusion of making decisions by choosing among fixed and limited alternatives designed by a management which deliberately leaves insignificant matters open to choice."[19]

Florida is not the first to see Einsteins everywhere he looks. In the early 1920s, the heyday of Taylorism, one true believer wrote that "the modern factory is a field of experiment constantly enlisting the worker in scientific research." Another wrote, "Our entire civilization is a system of physics, the simplest worker is a physicist."[20] (This is like calling a particle a particle physicist.) Florida's contribution is to update our view of these mini-Einsteins by taking a pop-existentialist view of their "creativity." It is a view that is familiar to most of us from kindergarten: creativity is a mysterious capacity that lies in each of us and merely needs to be "unleashed" (think finger painting). Creativity is what happens when people are liberated from the constraints of conventionality. According to this hippie theory, the personal grooming habits of Albert Einstein are highly significant—how else does one identify a "bizarre maverick operating at the bohemian fringe"?

The truth, of course, is that creativity is a by-product of mastery of the sort that is cultivated through long practice. It seems to be built up through *submission* (think a musician practicing scales, or Einstein learning tensor algebra). Identifying creativity with freedom harmonizes quite well with the culture of the new capitalism, in which the imperative of flexibility precludes dwelling in any task long enough to develop real competence. Such competence is the condition not only for genuine creativity but for economic independence such as the tradesman enjoys. So the liberationist ethic of what is sometimes called "the 1968 generation" perhaps paved the way for our increasing dependence. We're primed to respond to any invocation of the *aesthetics* of individuality. The *rhetoric* of freedom pleases our ears. The simulacrum of independent thought and action that goes by the name of "creativity" trips easily off the tongues of spokespeople for the corporate counterculture, and if we're not paying attention such usage might influence our career plans. The term invokes our powerful tendency to narcissism, and in doing so greases the skids into work that is not what we had hoped.

The Tradesman as Stoic

As against confused hopes for the transformation of work along emancipatory lines, we are recalled to the basic antagonism of economic life: work is toilsome and necessarily serves someone else's interests. That's why you get paid. Thus chastened, we may ask the proper question: What is it that we really want for a young person when we give him or her vocational advice? The only creditable answer, it seems to me, is one that avoids utopianism while keeping an eye on the human good: work that engages the human capacities as fully as possible. This humane and commonsensical answer goes against the central imperative of capitalism, which assiduously partitions thinking from doing. What is to be done? I offer no program, only an observation that might be of interest to anyone called upon to give guidance to the young.

Since manual work has been subject to routinization for over a century, the nonroutinized manual work that remains, outside the confines of the factory, would seem to be resistant to much further routinization. There still appear developments around the margins; for example, in the last twenty years prefabricated roof trusses and stairways have eliminated some of the more challenging elements from the jobs of framers who work for large tract developers, and prehung doors have done the same for finish carpenters generally. But still, the physical circumstances of the jobs performed by carpenters, plumbers, and auto mechanics vary too much for them to be executed by idiots; they require circumspection and adaptability. One feels like a man, not a cog in a machine. The trades are then a natural home for anyone who would live by his own powers, free not only of deadening abstraction but also of the insidious hopes and rising insecurities that seem to be endemic in our current economic life. Freedom from hope and fear is the Stoic ideal.

So what advice should one give to a young person? If you have a natural bent for scholarship; if you are attracted to the most difficult books out of an urgent need, and can spare four years to devote yourself to them, go to college. In fact, approach college in the spirit of craftsmanship, going deep into liberal arts and sciences. But if this is not the case; if the thought of four more years sitting in a classroom makes your skin crawl, the good news is that you don't have to go through the motions and jump through the hoops for the sake of making a decent living. Even if you *do* go to college, learn a trade in the summers. You're likely to be less damaged, and quite possibly better paid, as an independent tradesman than as a cubicle-dwelling tender of information systems or low-level "creative." To heed such advice would require a certain contrarian streak, as it entails rejecting a life course mapped out by others as obligatory and inevitable.

3

To Be Master of One's Own Stuff

Consider the case of a man who is told his car is not worth fixing. He is told this not by a mechanic but by a clipboard-wielding "service representative" at the dealership. Here is a layer of bureaucracy that makes impossible a conversation about the nitty-gritty of the situation. This man would gladly hover around the mechanic's bay and be educated about his car, but this is not allowed. The service representative represents not so much mechanical expertise as a position taken by an institution, and our spirited man is not sure he trusts this institution (maybe they want to sell him a new car). He hates the feeling of dependence, especially when it is a direct result of his not understanding something. So he goes home and starts taking the valve covers off his engine to investigate for himself. Maybe he has no idea what he is doing, but he trusts that whatever the problem is, he ought to be able to figure it out by his own efforts. Then again, maybe not—he may never get his valve train back together again. But he intends to go down swinging. Spiritedness, then, may be allied with *a spirit of in-*

quiry, through a desire to be *master of one's own stuff.* It is the prideful basis of self-reliance.

Often this kind of pride is in tension with one's own self-interest, considered narrowly—one is urged to consider the "opportunity costs" of fixing one's own car. "Time is money." This dictum is usually accompanied by a dim view of pride, as being at bottom a failure to appreciate one's true situation. (Thomas Hobbes regarded pride as a kind of false consciousness.) The idea of opportunity costs presumes the fungibility of human experience: all our activities are equivalent or interchangeable once they are reduced to the abstract currency of clock time, and its wage correlate. But, against the ever-expanding imperium of economics, we do well to insist on what we know firsthand, namely, the concrete heterogeneity of human experience—its apples-versus-oranges character. From an economistic mind-set, spiritedness or pridefulness appears as a failure to be properly calculative, which requires that one first be properly abstract. Economics recognizes only certain virtues, and not the most impressive ones at that. Spiritedness is an assertion of one's own dignity, and to fix one's own car is not merely to use up time, it is to have a different experience of time, of one's car, and of oneself.

It is characteristic of the spirited man that he takes an expansive view of the boundary of his own stuff—he tends to act as though any material things he uses are in some sense properly his, while he is using them—and when he finds himself in public spaces that seem contrived to break the connection between his will and his environment, as though he had no hands, this brings out a certain hostility in him. Consider the angry feeling that bubbles up in this person when, in a public bathroom, he finds himself waving his hands under the faucet, trying to elicit a few seconds of water from it in a futile rain dance of guessed-at mudras. This man would like to know: Why should there not be a *handle*? Instead he is asked to supplicate invisible powers.

It's true, some people fail to turn off a manual faucet. With its blanket presumption of irresponsibility, the infrared faucet doesn't merely respond to this fact, it *installs* it, giving it the status of normalcy. There is a kind of infantilization at work, and it offends the spirited personality.

To maintain decorum, the angry bathroom user does one of two things. He may seethe silently, succumbing to that self-division between inner and outer that is the mark of the defeated. In that case, the ratchet of his self-respect makes one more click in the wrong direction. Alternatively, he makes an effort to reevaluate his own response as unreasonable.[1] In either case, he is called upon to do a certain emotional work on himself. Often the murky fog of prescriptions that gets conveyed implicitly in our material culture would have us interpret as somehow *more rational* a state of being manually disengaged. More rational because more free.

There seems to be an ideology of freedom at the heart of consumerist material culture; a promise to disburden us of mental and bodily involvement with our own stuff so we can pursue ends we have freely chosen. Yet this disburdening gives us fewer occasions for the experience of direct responsibility. I believe the appeal of freedomism, as a marketing hook, is due to the fact it nonetheless captures something true. It points to a paradox in our experience of agency: to be master of your own stuff entails also being mastered by it.

The Motorcycle as Mule

Riding an early motorcycle entailed a certain preparation that went like this: Set the throttle at a very small opening (there would likely be no spring returning the throttle to idle position), set the choke at a position judged the appropriate one for the ambient temperature, and retard the spark timing manually. Then approach the kick-starter with due apprehension, bracing yourself for yet another blow to your chronically bruised shin. The thing about kick-starters is, they tend to kick back. This is especially likely if you don't retard the timing far enough, as then the motor backfires mechanically, as it were, through the kick-starter, sending your shin to its fated meeting with the foot peg. With the bike balanced on the center stand, and you on one foot, use your whole weight on the kick-starter to ease the motor slowly through its power stroke and well into its exhaust stroke, judged by listening for air escaping from the open exhaust valve. Having positioned the piston at the start of its intake stroke, you are ready to kick-start the bike. But first check to make sure there are no attractive women present to witness your display, nor any of your rivals, for it is likely to be a drama of strenuous impotence.

Before taking that first kick, it is traditional to light a cigarette and set it dangling at an angle that suggests nonchalance. While you're at it, send up a little prayer for fuel atomization. You wouldn't be riding a motorcycle if you weren't an optimist.

Ten or twelve kicks later, sweat dripping from your brow, you might get to ride the motorcycle. A quickening wind against your hot, flushed face is the reward for your labors. Sweeter still, the rush of acceleration carries you away from the scene you have made. But still you are not carefree. The spark timing must be adjusted manually for varying loads and engine speeds. What's more, the engine must be lubricated.

On Lubrication: From the Hand Pump to the Idiot Light, and Beyond

Writing in *Motor Cycling* in 1937, Phil Irving informs us that "In the early days," motorcycle designers "were content to fit a hand pump which, when operated by the rider, discharged a small amount of oil into the crankcase." Further,

> it must be admitted that, while engine speeds remained low and before aluminum replaced cast-iron as piston material, the system did work much better than one would expect. . . . Another reason for its success was that the rider could give the engine more or less oil as he thought fit, according to the work which it was doing. This is a valuable feature for a lubrication system to possess. . . . But the weak point of the manual system [was] that it was entirely dependent upon the rider's memory, and, in consequence, the forgetful man often

*let himself in for heavy repair bills, and the overcautious one
used about twice as much oil as necessary in his desire to
avoid such expense.[2]*

Early motorcycles were not very convenient. They may have
been more convenient than a horse (I can't say), but surely not
by much. More than today's machines, they made an issue of
certain intellectual and moral qualities of the rider; forgetfulness
and overcautiousness would show themselves when the rider applied oil "as he thought fit." One was drawn out of oneself and
into a struggle, by turns hateful and loving, with another thing
that, like a mule, was emphatically *not* simply an extension of
one's will. Rather, one had to conform one's will and judgment
to certain external facts of physics that still presented themselves *as* such. Old bikes don't flatter you, they educate you.

As every parent knows, infants think the world revolves
around them, and everything ought to be instantly available to
them. At an earlier stage of technological progress, I am sure
that contending with a motorcycle, like contending with the
farm animals that likely inhabited the same barn as the motorcycle, helped along the process of becoming an adult. When
your shin gets kicked, whether by a mule or a kick-starter, you
get schooled.

It would be strange to pine for the inconvenience of old
motorcycles. They truly are a pain in the ass. My point rather
is to consider the moral significance of material culture, and to
suggest that there are forces on the consumption side that parallel those we have seen on the production side. On all sides,
we see fewer occasions for the exercise of judgment, such as the

old-timers needed in riding their bikes. The necessity of such judgment calls forth human excellence. In the first place, the intellectual virtue of judging things rightly must be cultivated, and this is typically not the product of detached contemplation. It seems to require that the user of a machine have something at stake, an *interest* of the sort that arises through bodily immersion in some hard reality, the kind that kicks back. Corollary to such immersion is the development of what we might call a sub-ethical virtue: the user holds himself responsible to external reality, and opens himself to being schooled by it. His will is educated—both chastened and focused—so it no longer resembles that of a raging baby who knows only that he wants. Both as workers and as consumers, technical education seems to contribute to moral education.

The moral pedagogy that is tacit in material culture can take various forms. Consider an advertisement for a top-of-the-line Mercedes that appeared in the June 17, 2007, issue of the *New York Times Magazine*. The ad claimed that the car is "completely intuitive." This may or may not be true, but in any case the meaning of "intuitive" that is intended is fairly recent. It is the usage of those who design electronic equipment, and signifies something very different from what one would mean in uttering the same word while gazing at the stark engine compartment of, say, a 1963 VW Bug.

With electronic equipment, the facts of physics operate on such a scale that they do not present themselves to immediate experience for the user. The computer "interface" adds another layer of abstraction, as it screens the user also from the human-generated logic of the program running the software. Logic, like physics, is something hard and unyielding. The interface is meant to be "intuitive," meaning that it introduces as little psychic friction as possible between the user's intention and its realization. It is such resistance that makes one aware of reality as an independent thing. If all goes well, the user's dependence (on programmers who have tried to anticipate his every need when constructing the interface) remains well beneath his threshold of notice, and there is nothing to disturb his self-containment. The expanding empire of electronics *covers over* the mechanical.

How far we have come from the hand oiling of early motorcycles is indicated by the fact that some of the current Mercedes models do not even have a dipstick. This serves nicely as an index of the shift in our relationship to machines. If the oil level should get low, there is a very general exhortation that appears on a screen: "Service Required." Lubrication has been recast, for the user, in the frictionless terms of the electronic device. In those terms, lubrication has no rationale, and ceases to be an object of active concern for anyone but the service technician. In a sense, this increases the freedom of the Mercedes user. He has gained a kind of independence by not having to futz around with dipsticks and dirty rags.

But in another sense, it makes him more dependent. The burden of paying attention to his oil level he has outsourced to another, and the price he pays for this disburdenment is that he is entangled in a more minute, all-embracing, one might almost say maternal relationship with . . . what? Not with the service technician at the dealership, at least not directly, as there are layers of bureaucracy that intervene. Between driver and service tech lie corporate entities to which we attribute personhood only in the legal sense, as an abstraction: the dealership that employs the technician; Daimler AG, Stuttgart, Germany, who hold the service plan and warranty on their balance sheet; and finally Mercedes shareholders, unknown to one another, who collectively dissipate the financial risk of your engine running low on oil. There are now layers of collectivized, absentee interest in your motor's oil level, and no single person is responsible for it. If we understand this under the rubric of "globalization," we see that the tentacles of that wondrous animal reach down into things that were once unambiguously our own: the amount of oil in a man's crankcase.

It used to be that, in addition to a dipstick, you had also a very crude interface, simpler but no different conceptually from the sophisticated interface of the new Mercedes. It was called an "idiot light." One can be sure that the current system is not referred to in the Mercedes owner's manual as the "idiot system," as the harsh judgment carried by that term no longer makes any sense to us. By some inscrutable cultural logic, idiocy gets recast as something desirable.

It is important to understand that there has been no "high-tech" development such that it is no longer important to stay on top of oil consumption and leakage. With enough miles, oil is still consumed and will still leak; running low on oil will still trash the motor. There is nothing magical about the Mercedes, though such a superstition is encouraged by the absence of a dipstick. The facts of physics have not changed; what has changed is the place of those facts in our consciousness, and therewith the basic character of material culture.[3]

Agency versus Autonomy

Grime-under-the-fingernails, bodily involvement with the machines we use entails a kind of agency. Yet the decline of such involvement, through technological progress, is precisely the development that makes for an increase in *autonomy*. Is there a paradox here? Not having to futz around with machines, we are free to simply use them for our purposes. There seems to be a tension between a certain kind of agency and a certain kind of autonomy, and this is worth thinking about. My bike has an electric starter, and centrifugal spark advance, and an automatic oil pump, because I'd rather ride the bike than mess around with it. So I want to fully concede that such readiness to serve our will is a good attribute in a machine, in case there were any doubt.

But I also want to notice that there is a whole ideology of choice and freedom and autonomy, and that if one pays due attention, these ideals start to seem less like a bubbling up of the unfettered Self and more like something that is urged upon us. This becomes most clear in advertising, where Choice and Freedom and A World Without Limits and Master the Possibilities and all the other heady existentialist slogans of the consumerist Self are invoked with such repetitive urgency that they come to resemble a disciplinary system. Somehow, self-realization and freedom always entail buying something new, never conserving something old.

Thinking about manual engagement seems to require nothing less than that we consider what a human being is. That is, we are led to consider how the specifically human manner of being is lit up, as it were, by man's interaction with his world through his hands. For this a new sort of anthropology is called for, one that is adequate to our experience of agency. Such an account might illuminate the appeal of manual work in a way that is neither romantic nor nostalgic, but rather simply gives credit to the practice of building things, fixing things, and routinely tending to things, as an element of human flourishing.

The errors of freedomism may be illuminated by thinking about music. One can't be a musician without learning to play a particular instrument, subjecting one's fingers to the discipline of frets or keys. The musician's power of expression is founded upon a prior obedience; her musical agency is built up from an ongoing submission. To what? To her teacher, perhaps, but this is incidental rather than primary—there is such a thing as the self-taught musician. Her obedience rather is to the mechanical realities of her instrument, which in turn answer to certain natural necessities of music that can be expressed mathematically. For example, halving the length of a string under a given tension raises its pitch by an octave. These facts do not arise from the human will, and there is no altering them. I believe the example of the musician sheds light on the basic character of human agency, namely, that it arises only within concrete limits that are not of our making.[4]

These limits need not be physical; the important thing is rather that they are external to the self. Consider the experience of learning a foreign language, beautifully described by Iris Murdoch:

If I am learning, for instance, Russian, I am confronted by an authoritative structure which commands my respect. The task is difficult and the goal is distant and perhaps never entirely attainable. My work is a progressive revelation of something which exists independently of me. Attention is rewarded by a knowledge of reality. Love of Russian leads me away from myself towards something alien to me, something which my consciousness cannot take over, swallow up, deny or make unreal.[5]

In any hard discipline, whether it be gardening, structural engineering, or Russian, one submits to things that have their own intractable ways. Such hardness is at odds with the ontology of consumerism, which seems to demand a different conception of reality. The philosopher Albert Borgmann offers a distinction that clarifies this: he distinguishes between commanding reality and disposable reality, which corresponds to "things" versus "devices." The former convey meaning through their own inherent qualities, while the latter answer to our shifting psychic needs.

As an instance of "the eclipse of commanding reality and the prominence of disposable reality," Borgmann focuses on music. People play musical instruments a lot less than they used to; now we listen to the stereo or iPod. An instrument is "arduous to master and limited in its range," whereas a stereo is undemanding and makes every sort of music instantly available, granting us a kind of musical autonomy.

The stereo as a device contrasts with the instrument as a thing. A thing, in the sense in which I want to use the term,

*has an intelligible and accessible character and calls forth
skilled and active human engagement. A thing requires practice while a device invites consumption. Things constitute
commanding reality, devices procure disposable reality.*[6]

An example of "skilled and active human engagement"
might be a family gathered around a guitar, singing songs. This
would be an instance of what Borgmann calls a focal practice,
which is "the decided, regular, and normally communal devotion to a focal thing" (such as a guitar). Such things "gather our
world and radiate significance in ways that contrast with the di-
version and distraction afforded by commodities."[7]

Borgmann's categories help us to see that the tension between agency and autonomy can manifest in the meanings of
things themselves, or rather in our relationship to them.

The Betty Crocker Cruiser

I think most people have some awareness of the difference between active engagement and distracted consumption. In fact,
such an awareness seems to be used as a marketing hook by
advertisers, who know that we long for a lost authenticity in
our dealings with our own stuff. They have grasped that many
people feel bereft of the focal practices that used to be elicited
by certain objects, those that "gather our world and radiate significance."

An ad for the Yamaha Warrior in the July 2007 issue of
Motor Cyclist carries the caption "Life is what you make it. Start

making it your own." The picture shows a guy in his home shop, focused intently on his Warrior. There are motorcycle parts on shelves above his ancient workbench, and a full stack of grungy, obviously well-used tool boxes in standard mechanic's red. He's not smiling for the camera; he's lost in his work. A smaller caption reads, "The 102-cubic-inch fuel-injected Warrior. We build it. You make it your own." Smaller still, it reads, "You only get one shot at life—may as well make it mean something. And when you start with the four-time AMA Prostar Hot Rod Cruiser Class Champion Warrior, then add your choice of scores of Star Custom Accessories, the result is very powerful. *And* very personal."

So it turns out, in the small type, that what the guy is actually doing is attaching some accessory to his bike. This is a little like those model cars where the child's role consists of putting the decals on. Motorcycle culture retains a dim remembrance of the more involving character of the old machines, and the ad seems to gesture in that direction. Back in the 1950s, when the focal practice of baking was displaced by the advent of cake mix, Betty Crocker learned quickly that it was good business to make the mix not quite complete. The baker felt better about her cake if she was required to add an egg to the mix. So if the Warrior were to be christened with a street name, an apt one might be the Betty Crocker Cruiser, forged as it is in the Easy Bake Oven of consumerism.

With its system of Star Custom Accessories, Yamaha is following the lead of the automotive industry. Some years ago car manufacturers realized the profits being had in the aftermarket that serves the custom car scene and decided to, well, colonize it. So now, if you go to a Toyota dealership to look at a Scion (their cheaper, youth-oriented brand), you get a brochure full of pictures of crazy custom Scions, and profiles of the custom fabricators who have built them, typically with a welding helmet perched just so on their heads, and the obligatory wife beater.[8] The point is to sell a line of accessories, which can be combined in so many ways that one such combination is sure to capture "your unique personality." Notice the elision from agency (dude with welding helmet) to Personality, that is, the expressive Self, whose autonomy is realized in, indeed simply *is*, the array of Choice that lies open before him or her. But choosing is not creating, however much "creativity" is invoked in such marketing.

Displaced Agency

Countercultural people on the Left and Right alike complain about "the problem of technology." The complaint usually centers on our alleged obsession with control, as though the problem were the objectification of everything by a subject who is intoxicated with power, leading to a triumph of "instrumental rationality." But what if we are *inherently* instrumental, or pragmatically oriented, all the way down, and the use of tools is really fundamental to the way human beings inhabit the world? The ancient philosopher Anaxagoras wrote, "It is by having hands that man is the most intelligent of animals."[9] For the early Heidegger, "handiness" is the mode in which things in the world show up for us most originally: "the nearest kind of association is not mere perceptual cognition, but, rather, a handling, using, and taking care of things which has its own kind of 'knowledge.'"[10]

If these thinkers are right, then the problem of technology is almost the opposite of how it is usually posed: the problem is not "instrumental rationality," it is rather that we have come to live in a world that precisely does *not* elicit our instrumentality, the embodied kind that is original to us. We have too few occasions to *do* anything, because of a certain predetermination of things from afar.

It is precisely this experience of remote control that makes the spirited man angry; it offends the pride he takes in self-reliance. But this kind of response is perhaps becoming less common. The modern personality is being reorganized on a predicate of passive consumption, and it starts early in life. One of the hottest things at the shopping mall right now is a store called Build-a-Bear, where children are said to make their own teddy bears. I went into one of these stores, and it turns out that what the kid actually does is select the features and clothes for the bear on a computer screen, then the bear is made for him. Some entity has *leaped in* ahead of us and taken care of things already, with a kind of solicitude. The effect is to preempt cultivation of embodied agency, the sort that is natural to us.[11]

Children so preempted will be more well adjusted to emerging patterns of work and consumption. They are less likely to suffer the kind of agitation experienced by my hypothetical angry bathroom user. It will not strike them that there is anything amiss in the absence of a dipstick in the Mercedes.

What is this entity that leaps in on our behalf? It is something amorphous and difficult to name, but has about it something of *the public*. The activity of giving form to things seems to be increasingly the business of a collectivized mind, and from the standpoint of any particular individual, it feels like this forming has already taken place, somewhere else. In picking out your bear's features, or the options for your Warrior or Scion, you choose among the predetermined alternatives. Each of these alternatives offers itself as good. A judgment of its goodness has already been made by some dimly grasped others, otherwise it wouldn't be offered as an option in the catalogue. The consumer is disburdened not only of the fabrication, but of a basic *evaluative* activity. (For example, in customizing a car or motorcycle from scratch, the builder must harmonize aesthetic concerns with functional ones, and make compromises so the result isn't prone to, say, *catching on fire*.) The consumer is left with a mere decision. Since this decision takes place in a playground-safe field of options, the only concern it elicits is personal preference. The watchword here is easiness, as opposed to heedfulness. But because the field of options generated by market forces maps a collective consciousness, the consumer's vaunted freedom within it might be understood as a tyranny of the majority that he has internalized.

The market ideal of Choice by an autonomous Self seems to act as a kind of narcotic that makes the displacing of embodied agency go smoothly, or precludes the development of such agency by providing easier satisfactions. The growing dependence of individuals in *fact* is accompanied by ever more shrill invocations of freedom in *theory*, that is, in the ideology of consumerism. Paradoxically, we are narcissistic but not proud enough.

Yet consider the advertisement for the Warrior once again. Does it not present a contradiction, and thus point us in the right direction with a whisper? The ad is effective because it speaks to a deep discontent, and gives due credit to our nature as tool users, more than we give ourselves. Advertisers have constant recourse to a stock image: somebody engaged in some focal practice, lost in his work.[12] Often it is precisely that focal practice that the product promises to disburden us of, such as the building of a custom car or motorcycle. Such images present a picture of cultivated skill, the sort that makes possible some wholehearted activity. The marketers seem to grasp that it is not the product but the practice that is really attractive.

4

The Education of a Gearhead

A good diamond cutter has a different disposition than a good dog trainer. The one is careful, the other commanding. Different kinds of work attract different human types, and we are lucky if we find work that is fitting. There is much talk of "diversity" in education, but not much accommodation of the kind we have in mind when we speak about the quality of a man, or woman: the diversity of dispositions. We are preoccupied with demographic variables, on the one hand, and sorting into cognitive classes, on the other. Both collapse the human qualities into a narrow set of categories, the better to be represented on a checklist or a set of test scores. This simplification serves various institutional purposes. Fitting ourselves to them, we come to understand ourselves in light of the available metrics, and forget that institutional purposes are not our own. If the gatekeeper at some prestigious institution has opened a gate in front of us, we can't *not* walk through it. But as a young person surveys the various ways he could make a living, and how they might be part of a life well lived, the pertinent question *for him* may be not what IQ he has, but whether he is, for example, careful or commanding. If he is to find work that is fitting, he would do well to pause amid the general rush to the gates.

He might also take note of the funnel that surrounds him, by which I mean the use of psychiatric drugs to medicate boys, especially, against their natural bent toward action, the better to "keep things on track," as the school nurse says. This, too, serves institutional interests—I know because I taught high school briefly, and would have loved to set up a Ritalin fogger in my classroom, for the sake of order. It is a rare person who is naturally inclined to sit still for sixteen years in school, and then indefinitely at work, yet with the dismantling of high school shop programs this has become the one-size-fits-all norm, even as we go on about "diversity."

If different human types are attracted to different kinds of work, the converse is also true: the work a man does forms him. I have previously touched on the cognitive aspects of mechanical work; now I want to give a fuller portrait of the mechanic, connecting his manner of thinking to his manner of feeling. What, then, are the peculiar virtues and vices of the mechanic? I find the idea of "disposition" useful in thinking about the effect the work has had on me, and on other mechanics I have known. Or is it that people of a certain disposition are drawn to the work? In any case, the term captures something important I want to explore, namely, the mutual entanglement of intellectual qualities with moral qualities. This entanglement shows itself in the work we do.

The Would-be Apprentice

One of the first jobs I took outside the commune, at age fifteen, was at a Porsche repair shop in Emeryville, California.[1] At this time Emeryville was a mix of light industrial and black residential neighborhoods; my mother had recently bought a house there, and I was living with her. I used to walk by the shop and admire the 911s behind barbed wire in the adjoining yard. One day I walked in and asked for a job. The proprietor, whom I shall call Lance (not his real name), asked me what kind of skills I had. I told him about the electrical work I'd done, and a little carpentry as well. A woman in the commune who was a mechanic had taught me to do a basic tune-up. I didn't have much to offer, in other words.

Lance asked me to build an organizer for his desk, as a test of my abilities. We went to his office and he showed me what he had in mind: something that would sit at the back of his desk and span its width, with larger slots on the bottom and narrower ones on a second level. It had nothing to do with Porsches, but I took him up on the challenge and made the thing out of rosewood plywood in my mother's basement. Then I came by with samples of a couple different finishes on a scrap of the rosewood and let him pick the one he liked. I spent about a week on the project, and only charged him for the materials, which came to fifty-six dollars. I remember the amount because I was embarrassed at how much it had added up to. Should I not charge for the jar of stain, since there was quite a bit of it left? I decided I *would* charge him for the whole jar, and felt a rush of boldness in making this decision. This wasn't the commune, this was *business*, and that leftover stain was my profit. As absurdly timid as this decision sounds, it felt like self-assertion. It was exciting to be an entrepreneur, a capitalist rather than a communist; the vice of selfishness was suddenly a virtue.

Lance accepted the desk organizer and seemed happy enough with it. I was hired. I was given a locker and a set of coveralls that were way too big, with someone else's name stitched on a patch. Then I was given my first assignment. In retrospect, I think I must have expected this to consist of fondling a turbocharger, or perhaps licking Pirelli P7 tires (how many other fifteen-year-olds had this fetish in 1981?), because I remember the feeling I had when I was directed instead to the sink overflowing with dirty dishes upstairs. Lance lived above the shop, and his pad was a complete sty. I spent the first several days listlessly cleaning it, feeling hopeless and pissed off.[2]

Soon enough I moved on to a job on the first floor, in closer proximity to the Porsches. I had admired these cars for years, based on nothing more than their shape, the sound they made, and a vague mystique of fast; I didn't know much about their particulars (other than the tires). I was stationed at the parts cleaner, which looked a lot like the sink upstairs. But now, instead of using water that came out of a tap, I was using engine degreaser circulated by a pump and a stiff wire brush, with strict instructions that the brush was not to touch any gasket surfaces (for fear of marring them). The parts cleaner was located in a dark area between the well-lit shop proper, where the light-hits station KOIT-FM played on the speakers, and the fenced-in outside area. Here there was a rectangle of filthy concrete floor perhaps ten feet by twenty feet strewn with grimy parts, which needed to be cleaned. Initially, handling them was an experience of dissonance: these were Porsche parts, which I expected to be imbued with mystical qualities, yet here they were, covered in road grime. They didn't seem "high perform-ance," they seemed banal and shitty. I wasn't handling whale-tail spoilers with "Turbo Carrera" in elegant chrome script, I was handling transaxle support members and spindle carriers: the unseen stuff with unglamorous functions.

Lance would periodically have me take some of these cleaned parts and spray-paint them black. Then he would install them on cars, and take pictures of the "new" parts in place. It became clear that in stepping off the reservation of the commune and into the world of commerce, there were some psychic adjust-ments I was going to have to make.

Lance and I weren't yet sure what to make of one another, and I took it as an invitation to get acquainted when he asked me to come along as he test-drove a 911 on which he had just done the brakes. I had never actually ridden in a Porsche before. We were going to ride across town and pick up some clutch parts over on Fourth Street in Berkeley. We got in the car, and for the first time I heard the distinctive exhaust note of the Porsche flat six as the driver does, transmitted to the interior, with the sharp edges of the raspy growl rounded off to a rum-ble. I rolled down the window to better hear the motor's music. We pulled out of the shop and accelerated hard down the street. Lance suddenly seemed very much in his element. We're screaming now, still accelerating in third gear, and we're com-ing up on the cross section with San Pablo Avenue, a busy thoroughfare. We're getting *really* close, and we're still going *really* fast. I realize Lance simply isn't going to stop. Incredulous, my right foot starts stabbing at the air involuntarily, searching for a brake pedal. About fifteen yards before the crosswalk, Lance hits the brakes. The car just squats down on all fours and stops, as though a giant hand had reached out and pressed us into the pavement right . . . *here*. I never imagined there could be brakes like that.

From the Powell Street entrance we got on the freeway, Interstate 80. There was lots of late-afternoon traffic, and Lance was having his way with it, darting in and out, leaving inches between cars. Initially I was scandalized that he was doing this with a customer's car, but his confidence was absolute, and apparently just, so I started to relax. This was the first time I had ridden with someone with racetrack experience, and it was exhilarating. (The shop campaigned a Porsche 930 as well as a 356 at Laguna Seca, the road racing course down in Monterey.)

There were two mechanics in addition to Lance: a Mexican guy and a white guy. One day the white guy was doing a brake job on a 911 that was up on the lift, and Lance told him to teach me something. So the white guy showed me how to pack a wheel bearing: you get a big dollop of grease on the heel of your hand, then press the bearing into it. The grease comes oozing up through the ball bearings, between the inner and outer races. Then you rotate the bearing a little and repeat, working your way around the circumference. Once you've gone all the way around, you turn the bearing over and force the grease in from the opposite side. It's an important job; a wheel bearing that isn't adequately packed with grease will wear quickly, overheat, and eventually fail by either seizing or coming apart, either of which could cause a wreck. But beyond this simple lesson I didn't learn much, and mostly did menial work. Lance didn't have much interest in being a mentor. With or without a mentor, however, my mechanical education could no longer be put off, since my own car, a 1963 VW Bug, needed constant attention.

String Theory

Working on my car without guidance, I felt constantly thwarted. Corroded nuts and bolts routinely broke or would round off; I came to be surprised when they simply loosened. Intermittent electrical gremlins eluded diagnosis. How much of this was due to the rat's nest of decaying, somehow organic-looking wiring behind the dash? From what I'd read, some "drivability" problems (sputtering, flat spots, hesitation) pointed to carburetor issues but could just as well be attributed to the ignition system. A lot seemed to depend on the weather. The car mocked my efforts to get a handle on it, as though it obeyed some evil genius rather than rational principles.

Meanwhile, I was getting reacquainted with my father, living with him after six years away in the commune and another year living with my mother. A physicist, he would sometimes proffer some bit of scientific knowledge that was meant to be helpful as I sat on the ground in front of my lifeless engine. These nuggets rarely seemed to pan out. One day as I came into the house filthy, frustrated, and reeking of gasoline, my dad looked up from his chair and said to me, out of the blue, "Did you know you can always untie a shoelace just by pulling on one end, even if it's in a double knot?" I didn't really know what to do with this information. It seemed to be coming from a different universe than the one I was grappling with.

Thinking about that posited shoelace now, it occurs to me maybe you can and maybe you can't untie it at a stroke—it depends. If the shoelace is rough and spongy, and the knot is tight, it will be a lot harder to undo than if the knot is loose and the shoelace is made of something slick and incompressible, like silk ribbon. The shoelace might well break before it comes undone. He was speaking of a *mathematical* string, which is an idealized shoelace, but the idealization seemed to have replaced any actual shoelace in his mind as he got wrapped up in some theoretical problem. As a teenager, this substitution wasn't yet clear to me as such. But it began to dawn on me that my father's habits of mind, as a mathematical physicist, were ill suited to the reality I was dealing with in an old Volkswagen.

Yet he seemed to know what he was doing, as a scientist. This seemed like a contradiction. Weren't we dealing with the same physical reality? The dissonance between his utterances and my experiences planted the seeds of a philosophical reflection that would come to fruition only twenty years later. The immediate effect was that I started to become a bit of a fatalist. I remember my friend John, who had his own travails with American muscle cars, once asking me about the design of the VW Bug. I must have had an especially frustrating day, because the words came hissing out of my mouth: "Design?! Nobody *designed* it." The car seemed a brute fact in the world, impervious to my will and my efforts to comprehend it. The ancient Greek poet Solon captured this feeling when he suggested that Fate is more powerful than any technical knowledge; it "makes all human effort fundamentally insecure, however earnest and logical it may seem to be."[3] The feeling of being subject to fate chastens the conceit of mastery. This might make a person humble, but in my own case the humility had an edge to it. As I groped my way toward a modus vivendi with the Bug, I took my new fatalism to be a stinging rebuke to the pretense of easy intellectual mastery that my father was offering. So my own sense of impotence was weirdly delicious; it was based on a truer self-awareness than my father possessed, as I saw it.

To repeat a point I made earlier, modern science adopts an otherworldly ideal of how we come to know nature: through mental constructions that are more intellectually tractable than material reality, and in particular amenable to mathematical representation.[4] Through such renderings we become masters of nature. Yet the kind of thinking that begins from idealizations such as the frictionless surface and the perfect vacuum sometimes fails us (as my dad's advice failed me), because it isn't sufficiently involved with the particulars. Precisely because such thinking enjoys all the credit and authority of science, however, when it fails us we may be tempted to see obscurity and unreason everywhere ("nobody *designed* it"), and even take pleasure in such obscurity. This reactionary tendency is a natural response to the pretense of modern reason. The reaction has an adolescent quality to it; there is a secret kinship between modernism and anti-modernism that just happens to mirror my relationship with my father.

At this point I hated my car, but also loved it. It was the source of my mobility and independence, as well as the pure pleasure of driving. So it was a passionate, dysfunctional relationship, the sort one can't simply walk away from. I had no choice but to stay engaged with the car. This struggle has persisted throughout my life, recurring under the hoods of cars or while sitting on a milk crate in front of a bike that has me stumped. What I have learned is that mechanical work has a chancy, elusive character, very different from mathematics, even for expert mechanics.

Aristotle can help here. He expanded the idea of an art, or *techne*, to include those cases where our efforts are less than fully effective. In doing so, he steers a course between impotent fatalism and its opposite, a fantasy of complete mastery, shedding light on the true character of human agency.

Some arts reliably attain their object—for example, the art of building. If the building falls down, one can say in retrospect that the builder didn't know what he was doing. But there is another class of arts that Aristotle calls "stochastic." An example is medicine. Mastery of a stochastic art is compatible with failure to achieve its end (health). As Aristotle writes, "It does not belong to medicine to produce health, but only to promote it as much as is possible. . . ."[5] Fixing things, whether cars or human bodies, is very different from building things from scratch. The mechanic and the doctor deal with failure every day, even if they are expert, whereas the builder does not. This is because the things they fix are *not of their own making*, and are therefore never known in a comprehensive or absolute way. This experience of failure tempers the conceit of mastery; the doctor and the mechanic have daily intercourse with the world as something independent, and a vivid awareness of the difference between self and nonself. Fixing things may be a cure for narcissism.

Like building houses, mathematics is *constructive*; every element is fully within one's view, and subject to deliberate placement. In a sense, then, a mathematical representation of the world renders the world as something of our own making. Substituting mathematical strings for shoelaces entails a bit of self-absorption, and skepticism, too: the world is interesting and intelligible only insofar as we can reproduce it in ideal form, as a projection from our selves. By contrast, in diagnosing and fixing things made by others (this other may be Volkswagen, God, or Natural Selection), one is confronted with obscurities, and must remain constantly open to the signs by which they reveal themselves. This openness is incompatible with self-absorption; to maintain it we have to fight our tendency to get anchored in snap judgments. This is easier said than done.[6]

Because the stochastic arts diagnose and fix things that are variable, complex, and not of our own making, and therefore not fully knowable, they require a certain disposition toward the thing you are trying to fix. This disposition is at once cognitive and moral. Getting it right demands that you be *attentive* in the way of a conversation rather than *assertive* in the way of a demonstration.[7] I believe the mechanical arts have a special significance for our time because they cultivate not creativity, but the less glamorous virtue of attentiveness. Things need fixing and tending no less than creating.

. . .

During those interludes when the Bug ran, I acquired a taste for driving sideways. In a rear-engine car, you can easily make the tail slide, especially if it has a swing axle suspension. You go fast into a corner, lift off the throttle to unweight the back, the rear swings to the outside, you get back on the throttle to keep the tires spinning while steering into the slide, and you find yourself driving sideways. With a little practice this can be done with pretty good control, and it's a lot of fun. I liked to do it on city streets, on my way to Berkeley High School in the morning. Or I'd head to the parking lot of the Claremont Hotel after it rained. This lot was spacious, and there was a spot where I could keep the parked Jaguars and Mercedes to the inside of my arc, most of them anyway. This is good because when things get out of hand, the risk is always on the outside. I'd sometimes lock eyes with some startled matron, keys in hand, as I came round the bend at full drift, a skinny kid with poofy hair and a demonic grin.

In keeping with this pursuit, I installed a roll cage, gas shocks, and some decent tires. But by 1983, when I was seventeen, the car had developed low compression in one cylinder. A 1200 cc flat four, the motor had once claimed forty horsepower, which is not much of a claim to begin with. Now in its decrepitude, it risked making ridiculous the rest of the car. Or perhaps *more* ridiculous. Something needed to be done. I spent the end of that summer waiting to hear a sound that was long overdue: the unmuffled, "race only," "not legal for highway use in the State of California" note of Charles Martin's early-1960s

VW bus. When I finally heard it for sure, I rushed to the driveway. Here, finally, was Chas to deliver my new motor.

The Mentor

The ex-boyfriend of an older housemate, Chas was a machinist by training. Currently he worked the parts counter at Donsco, the oldest VW speed shop in the Bay Area, in Belmont. He also built race motors for them and pitted for their off-road racing campaigns. Once a classical guitar-playing Buddhist vegetarian, he was now a gun freak and brilliant misanthropist. He still had long hair, but it was rarely released from the bun under his tweed cap.

His orange bus, with wheel wells cut away to accommodate large off-road tires in the back, was a chaotic treasure trove of superb American handguns, Snap-on tools, and VW parts. The darkness behind the cab carried a sharp note of Berryman's B-12 Chemtool on top of a more subtle smell that is generic to mechanics—a mixed-up aroma of various petroleum distillates that had been oxidized by combustion, thickened with road grime, and ripened on a substrate of shop rags to the point of acquiring substance. He kept a large tank of CO_2 in his bus for running an air impact wrench, indispensable for swapping out the transaxle on a race car in the desert. This bus was his only personal space, and at this time cell phones were something you saw only in the movies. Outside Donsco business hours, you reached Chas by calling the Lyons restaurant in San Mateo, where he manned a certain stool at one end of the coffee counter.

Oppressed in my seventeen-year-old way by the liberal pieties of Berkeley, I had recently taken to wearing combat boots and reading *Soldier of Fortune* magazine. But Chas was something different, the first genuine reactionary I ever met. Deeply cynical and witty, he loosened these angry tendencies of mine with his corrosive humor. He also initiated me into a certain positive possibility opened up by alienation from all things respectable: the pleasures of *metal.*

Of course, wood is great. But to this young man it seemed that wood was for hippies, and hippies in various guises ruled the world. The wood whisperer with his hand planes, his curly maple, and his workshop on Walden Pond is a stock alter ego of gentlefolk everywhere, and I wanted none of it. A grade 10.9 nylock nut, on the other hand, is appreciated only after a certain initiation, one that tends away from the mysticism of the official counterculture. It is a strictly utilitarian mentality bred in the crucible of motor sports, where every component is stressed up to and beyond its limit. The failure of metal parts had always seemed to me a mere hypothetical possibility, an abstract preoccupation of engineers, but for Chas it was a daily reality. Two bolts, for example, that looked identical to me represented for him the difference between glory and catastrophe. There is a glyphlike code of markings on fasteners that indicates their country of origin, as well as their grading. Categorically, the best steel is American steel (at least, it was in 1983). So the motor-sport mentality fits easily with a certain nativism. This is based not on racial animosity, but on such considerations as tensile strength and resistance to torque shear. (The cosmopolitan tends to live remote from such considerations.)

For real gearheads, the grade of metal in this utilitarian sense gets imbued with an aesthetic charge as well, perhaps because the end served by the component is at bottom not utilitarian at all, but rather spiritual: the need for speed. Far from practical, this is the kind of need that bankrupts those who heed the noble call.

You can quadruple the amount of horsepower a VW engine makes, or even more, if you need it to last only for a single race and are willing to spend absurd amounts of time and money building it. I was reminded of this by Chas when we first discussed what was to be done about my engine situation. Scrawled above the dingy parts counter at Donsco was a slogan: "Speed costs. How fast do you want to spend?" It represented a kind of anti-salesmanship. If the usual method of the salesman is to insinuate himself into your favor, play on your hopes, and lead you imperceptibly to an expensive decision, the mechanics behind the counter at any old-school speed shop seem to adopt a more ambivalent stance, in which the desire to sell is counterpoised with haughty professionalism. If you want chromed "bolt on" baubles that claim to give you power, go to a chain auto parts store to indulge your shallow fantasies. Then put the sticker on your rear window. If, on the other hand, you want to go deep and have your crank journals nitrided, you've come to the right place. Just tear down your motor and bring us the crank. This Olympian stance can have a powerful effect on the customer. It hints at the existence of an exclusive club that he might aspire to be a member of (those who have held a bare crankshaft in their hands). So perhaps the disdain one encounters in speed shops is a higher form of salesmanship, the kind that announces a hierarchy of human beings. But you can't buy entry to this world, you have to earn it. There is no sticker.

Chas was a good man, and he didn't want to be responsible for starting me down this path. Though he tried to warn me against the speed mentality, his whole life was a repudiation of such sobriety. The sheer perversity of making a VW go fast attracts a different human type than the type who is attracted to cars that are supposed to go fast. Chas clearly had a kink in his soul, and suddenly the world was a less lonely place for me.

After briefly flirting with the "hand grenade" option, which might have made 150 horsepower but would be lucky to last 20,000 miles before blowing up, and cost more to build than I had, we agreed to build a "mild" motor, one that could be expected to last 100,000 miles but still lighted up Chas's eyes. He promised it would be "a screamer." I spent to the tune of about 80 horsepower. First, the purchasable stuff: a crank with a 69 mm stroke, forged pistons to fit an 87 mm bore, a temperamental but voluptuous double-barrel Italian carburetor capable of full-throated arias, free-flow exhaust, a German centrifugal advance distributor, a remote oil cooler and full-flow filter, a lightened flywheel, and a heavy clutch. Just as important: some careful assembly work by Chas. The total parts bill came to $800, and Chas's labor bill was another $800. I got the money from my grandfather.

Chas agreed to let me "help" him build the motor, that is, to stand around and get in the way, mostly, while he taught me things. Under his supervision I match-ported the intake manifolds to the intake ports on the cylinder heads. My first task was to file down the metal gasket that joins the two parts with a half-round file, to match the intake ports exactly. I then used the custom-fit gasket as a template for the intake manifolds: after painting machinist's blue dye on the manifold flange, I used the tip of an X-acto knife to trace the outline of the gasket on the flange (the blue dye makes the scored line more visible). I then removed metal on the manifolds, using a pneumatic die grinder that spins at 25,000 rpm, and blended the new shape farther up into the manifold. The point is to match the shapes of the two passageways where they meet, eliminating discontinuities

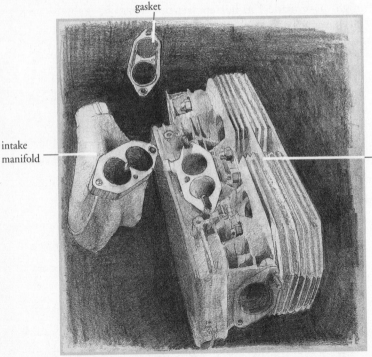

gasket

intake
manifold

cylinder
head

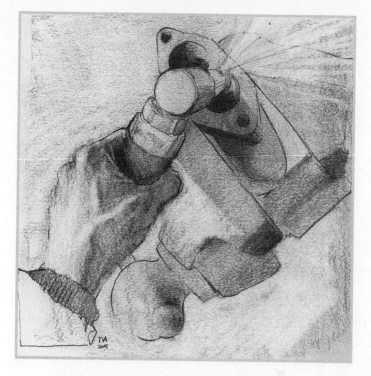

Grinding the intake manifold

that could introduce turbulence and compromise flow. We wanted this motor to breathe.

Forensic Wrenching

Match-porting is one small part of what is called "blue printing" an engine: by careful measuring and hand fitting, the motor can be brought to a higher level of precision than is achieved when you take for granted the fit of aftermarket parts—for example, these intake manifolds—where there is no consistent engineering intention among the various manufacturers. Someone building a high-performance motor combines parts from different makers, so he has to be something of an engineer himself, often modifying parts; there is nobody else in charge of making it all work together properly. (And in fact it is common for "high performance" engines to perform wretchedly, worse than stock.)

Blue printing is an extremely time-consuming process, and it is difficult to say where careful assembly ends and blue printing begins, since rebuilding old motors involves lots of measuring and judging to begin with. The wear of each part must be determined so you can calculate whether tolerances are within spec. This involves visual inspection as well as measuring; the skills of an engine builder are in good part forensic. After some time in the solvent tank and some elbow grease, followed by hot soapy water, the internals of the torn-down motor were spotlessly clean. Chas then looked for signs of galling and discoloration that would indicate excessive heat, hence inadequate lubrication, or some other source of unacceptable friction. In fact there was some galling on the cam lobes, and the task now was to identify the root cause.

Root causes manifest as coherent *patterns* of wear, and knowledge of these patterns disciplines the perception of an engine builder; his attentiveness has a certain direction to it. He is not just passively receptive to data, but actively seeks it out. Pursuing one hypothesis, Chas looked for mushrooming at the tips of the valve stems, which bear on the cam lobes via rocker arms, push rods, and lifters. Sure enough, some of the valve stems were slightly bulged out at their tips. Previously, as we were cleaning parts, I had held one of these valves in my hand and examined it naïvely, but had not noticed the mushrooming. Now I saw it. Countless times since that day, a more experienced mechanic has pointed out to me something that was right in front of my face, but which I lacked the knowledge to see. It is an uncanny experience; the raw sensual data reaching my eye before and after are the same, but without the pertinent framework of meaning, the features in question are invisible. Once they have been pointed out, it seems impossible that I should not have seen them before.

This weird aspect of perception was brought home to me twenty years later in a drawing class, and the parallels between mechanical perception and drawing merit a digression here. The teacher of the class, who happened to be my shop mate and fellow motorcycle mechanic Tommy, brought a human skeleton for us to draw. I drew what could only be described as a Halloween display such as you might see at Walgreens. I had seen images of skeletons since I was a little kid, and try as I might to represent the skeleton before me, I drew an icon of the thing rather than the thing itself. To actually reproduce the pattern of light hitting your eye with a pencil seems like it should be a straightforward matter, but it is extraordinarily difficult. It seems to require that you short-circuit your normal mode of perception, which is less data-driven than concept-driven. We have an *idea* of the thing that, in a sense, pre-constitutes the thing for us, prior to sensual experience.

In a sort of empiricist shock therapy, Tommy turned the skeleton so that we were viewing it end-on, with the pelvis toward us. Now we were viewing it in a completely unaccustomed perspective, with most of its familiar features foreshortened or obscured. But those features were still present in my mind, and because they were now so completely inappropriate to the way the skeleton was actually presenting itself to me, their interference in my attempt to draw what I saw became more obvious, an object of attention. Trying to draw the skeleton end-on required going back and forth: first a critical attention by which I tried to be aware of, and hold in abeyance, my prior Hal-

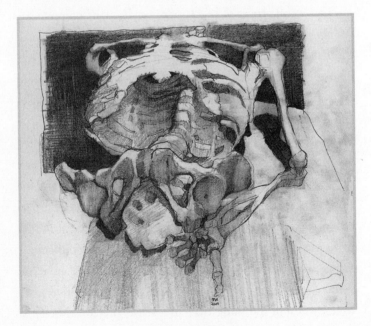

Skeleton viewed end-on

loween skeleton, then trying to attend to the visual data more directly. But the latter activity was like trying to bushwhack through a thick undergrowth of perception, with no apparent way forward to comprehension. Lines and planes were not clearly distinguishable in the jumble of bones, nor was there an evident logic of function such as you see in a skeleton as normally viewed, or in the framing of a house before the sheathing is nailed up. It wasn't so much that it felt like there was too much information, but rather that what I saw was ambiguous, unstructured, uncodable. Trying to represent it was exhausting, and seemed to demand not just mental stamina but something more fundamental. Iris Murdoch writes that good art

often seems to us mysterious because it resists the easy patterns of the fantasy, whereas there is nothing mysterious about the forms of bad art since they are the recognizable and familiar rat-runs of selfish day-dream. Good art shows us how difficult it is to be objective by showing us how differently the world looks to an objective vision.[8]

Pursuing his hypothesis about the galling on the cam lobes further, Chas took one of the valve springs and, with my extra pair of hands, clamped it in a vise together with an ancient bathroom scale that had once been white and was now black. Using a vernier caliper to measure spring compression, he had me close the vise until the caliper reading corresponded to the installed height of the valve minus the maximum valve opening. The reading on the bathroom scale was higher than it

Measuring spring compression

should have been. I distinctly recall Chas clucking with satisfaction. "Yep. As I thought." To accommodate higher rpms, the previous owner, a known shade tree performance enthusiast, had installed stiffer valve springs, which put more friction on the cam lobes. In twenty years, my motor had been subjected to who knows how many such interventions. It had been the site of focused attention by others, and its present state represented the layers of their varying purposes, gathered together in a material thing. The forensic efforts of a skilled engine builder are thus a kind of human archaeology.

Volkswagens in particular, as the People's Car, tend to get passed around like a reasonably priced sex worker, and it is rare to find one that hasn't been pawed at by a train of users applying more urgency than finesse. The story that unfolds in the course of rehabilitating a VW engine can take different twists. It may have been subjected to clumsy, boyish innocence, such as my predecessor surely felt in his heart as he ripped open his package from JC Whitney and held the brand-new "high performance" valve springs in his hand, then proceeded to drive the reciprocating parts harder and faster, without any heed to the motor's lubrication issues. Or it may be a tale of appalling moral squalor, as when it becomes evident that the previous owner failed to change the oil, like, ever.

Rebuilding a motor, then, is more humanly involved than assembling one on an assembly line. It is a craft activity. But what does this mean, exactly? We have seen that a mechanic's perception is not that of a spectator. It is an active process, bound up with his knowledge of patterns and root causes. Further, his knowledge and perception are bound up with a third thing, which is a kind of ethical involvement. He looks for clues and causes only if he *cares* about the motor, in a personal way.

Personal Knowledge

We usually think of intellectual virtue and moral virtue as being very distinct things, but I think they are not. The mutual entanglement of ethics and cognition was captured by Robert Pirsig in what is to my mind the best (and funniest) passage in *Zen and the Art of Motorcycle Maintenance*. The narrator's bike's engine has seized up at high speed, a disconcerting experience that causes the rear wheel to lock up. Not wishing to get involved in a big mechanical hassle himself, he takes the bike to a shop.

> *The shop was a different scene from the ones I remembered. The mechanics, who had once all seemed like ancient veterans, now looked like children. A radio was going full blast and they were clowning around and talking and seemed not to notice me. When one of them finally came over he barely listened to the piston slap before saying, "Oh yeah. Tappets."*[9]

Three overhauls, some haphazard misdiagnoses, and a lot of bad faith later, the narrator picks up his bike from the shop for the final time.

> *[N]ow there really was a tappet noise. They hadn't adjusted them. I pointed this out and the kid came with an open-end adjustable wrench, set wrong, and swiftly rounded both of the sheet-aluminum tappet covers, ruining both of them.*
> *"I hope we've got some more of those in stock," he said.*
> *I nodded.*
> *He brought out a hammer and cold chisel and started to pound them loose. The chisel punched through the aluminum cover and I could see he was pounding the chisel*

right into the engine head. On the next blow he missed the chisel completely and struck the head with the hammer, breaking off a portion of two of the cooling fins.[10]

Finally he gets on the road, only to discover that the shop had neglected to bolt the engine back into the frame; it was hanging on by a single bolt.

I found the cause of the seizures a few weeks later, waiting to happen again. It was a little twenty-five-cent pin in the internal oil-delivery system that had been sheared and was preventing oil from reaching the head at high speeds.

. . . Why did they butcher it so? . . . They sat down to do a job and they performed it like chimpanzees. Nothing personal in it.

. . . But the biggest clue seemed to be their expressions. They were hard to explain. Good-natured, friendly, easygoing— and uninvolved. They were like spectators. You had the feeling they had just wandered in there themselves and somebody had handed them a wrench. There was no identification with the job. No saying, "I am a mechanic."[11]

"Nothing personal in it." Here is a paradox. On the one hand, to be a good mechanic seems to require personal commitment: I am a mechanic. On the other hand, what it means to be a good mechanic is that you have a keen sense that you answer to something that is the opposite of personal or idiosyncratic; something universal. In Pirsig's story, there is an underlying fact: a sheared-off pin has blocked an oil gallery, resulting in oil starvation to the head and excessive heat, causing the seizures. This is the Truth, and it is the same for everyone. But finding this truth requires a certain disposition in the individual: attentiveness, enlivened by a sense of responsibility to the motorcycle. He has to internalize the well working of the motorcycle as an object of passionate concern. The truth does not reveal itself to idle spectators.

Pirsig's mechanic is, in the original sense of the term, an idiot. Indeed, he exemplifies the truth about idiocy, which is that it is at once an ethical and a cognitive failure. The Greek *idios* means "private," and an *idiōtēs* means a private person, as opposed to a person in their public role—for example, that of motorcycle mechanic. Pirsig's mechanic is idiotic because he fails to grasp his public role, which entails, or should, a relation of active concern to others, and to the machine. He is not involved. It is not his problem. Because he is an idiot.

This still comes across in the related English words "idiomatic" and "idiosyncratic," which similarly suggest self-enclosure. For example, when a foreigner asks him for directions, the idiot will reply idiomatically, rather than refer to a shared coordinate system. He also lacks the attentive openness that seeks things out in the shared world, as when Pirsig's mechanic "barely listened to the piston slap before saying, 'Oh yeah. Tappets.'" At bottom, the idiot is a solipsist.[12]

The forensic perceptual expertise of the engine builder is active in the sense that he knows what he is looking for. But with the idiot we see the result of a premature conceit of knowledge. If the expert and the idiot both know what they are looking for, what is the difference between them? How does the disposition of the one give rise to expertise, while the other rushes in and habitually finds himself in such straits that he ends up applying cold chisels to cylinder heads?

Seeing Clearly, or Unselfishly

The cognitive psychologists speak of "metacognition," which is the activity of stepping back and thinking about your own thinking. It is what you do when you stop for a moment in your pursuit of a solution, and wonder whether your understanding of the *problem* is adequate. Contrary to the cognitive psychologists' own view of the matter (or rather, outside the purview of their discipline as they conceive it), this cognitive capacity seems to be rooted in a moral capacity. It isn't captured by the psychometrician's IQ tests, nor by the reductive view of intelligence as mental "processing power," as though the data of experience were simply *given* to us, the way they are to a computer, ready for processing. In the real world, problems do not present themselves unambiguously. Piston slap may indeed sound like loose tappets, so to be a good mechanic you have to be constantly attentive to the possibility that you may be mistaken. This is an ethical virtue.

Iris Murdoch writes that to respond to the world justly, you first have to perceive it clearly, and this requires a kind of "unselfing." "[A]nything which alters consciousness in the direction of unselfishness, objectivity and realism is to be connected with virtue."[13] "[V]irtue is the attempt to pierce the veil of selfish consciousness and join the world as it really is."[14] This attempt is never fully successful, because we are preoccupied with our own concerns. But getting outside her own head is the task the artist sets herself, and this is the mechanic's task, too. Both, if they are good, use their imagination "not to escape the world but to join it, and this exhilarates us because of the distance between our ordinary dulled consciousness and an apprehension of the real."[15] This is the exhilaration a mechanic gets when he finds the underlying cause of some problem. There seems to be a connection between the idiotic Halloween skeleton that I drew and the idiotic mechanic's misdiagnosis of Pirsig's motor. Likewise, there is a connection between the skeleton that Tommy drew and Chas's discovery of the root cause of the worn cam lobes.

Any discipline that deals with an authoritative, independent reality requires honesty and humility. I believe this is especially so of the stochastic arts that fix things, such as doctoring and wrenching, in which we are not the makers of the things we tend. Similarly, in art that is representational, the artist holds herself responsible to something not of her making. If we fail to respond appropriately to these authoritative realities, we remain idiots. If we succeed, we experience the pleasure that comes with progressively more acute vision, and the growing sense that our actions are fitting or just, as we bring them into conformity with that vision. This conformity is achieved in an iterated back-and-forth between seeing and doing. Our vision is improved by acting, as this brings any defect in our perception to vivid awareness.

Idiocy as an Ideal

If occasions for the exercise of judgment are diminished, the moral-cognitive virtue of attentiveness will atrophy. The institutionalized carelessness of Taylorized work, from the assembly line to the electronic sweatshop, would reform us all in the image of Pirsig's idiot. We have to wonder, then, whether degraded work entails not just dumbing down but also a certain unintended moral reeducation. Recall that shortly after the advent of the assembly line, one observer noted that

> *Scientific managers . . . have complained bitterly of the poor and lawless material from which they must recruit their workers, compared with the efficient and self-respecting craftsmen who applied for employment twenty years ago.*[16]

We have all had the experience of dealing with a service provider who seems to have been reduced to a script-reading automaton. We have also heard the complaints of employers about not being able to find conscientious workers. Are these two facts perhaps related? There seems to be a vicious circle in which degraded work plays a pedagogical role, forming workers into material that is ill suited for anything but the overdetermined world of careless labor.

These thoughts should inform our choices as consumers. It may or may not make sense to have an engine rebuilt by your local mechanic, in narrow economic terms. You may be better off buying a rebuilt engine from one of the chain auto parts stores, which get them from high-volume remanufacturing operations down in Mexico. These factories simply ignore the finer points that engage a mechanic's attention. (That's why they typically have a warranty of only 12,000 miles, or 36,000 at most.) But a more public-spirited calculus would include a humane regard for the kind of labor involved in each alternative: on the one side disciplined attentiveness, enlivened by a mechanic's own judgments and ethical entanglement with a motor, and on the other systematized carelessness. Further, the decision is inherently political, because the question *who benefits* is at stake: the internationalist order of absentee capital, or an individual possessed of personal knowledge. Given the ever-bolder raids of capital into the psychic territory of labor, our consumer choices contribute to a land war, on one side or the other, whether we are aware of the fact or not. This can be understood by analogy with our food choices: having a motor rebuilt would correspond roughly to the decision to buy food from a local farmer versus a distant agribusiness. This is a practice the bohemian consumer already has in the cultural tool kit he uses, not only to construct his dissident self image but to give expression to his genuine public-spiritedness. If the regard that many people now have for the wider ramifications of their food choices could be brought to our relationships to our own automobiles, it would help sustain pockets of mindful labor.

Obviously, not every mechanic carries a countercultural dagger in his boot like Chas. But by the mere fact that they stand ready to fix things, as a class they are an affront to the throwaway society. Just as important, the kind of thinking they do, if they are good, offers a counterweight to the culture of narcissism.

5

The Further Education of a Gearhead:
From Amateur to Professional

The moral-cognitive failure exemplified by the idiotic mechanic is something I have experienced more times than I care to recall, and I continue to commit acts of idiocy upon motorcycles to this day. But less often, I think. I want to consider how working on other people's bikes, for pay, can help along the process of "unselfing" described by Iris Murdoch. To respond to the world justly, you have to see it clearly, and for this you have to get outside your own head. Knowing you're going to have to explain your labor bill to a customer accomplishes just this.

Allow me to briefly run through the sequence of events that led me to go into business fixing motorcycles. Chas ended up joining the army. I went to UC Santa Barbara for college, and got introduced to philosophy in my senior year. It was a jolt of clarity. Graduating with a degree in physics, I couldn't find a job based on that credential, so I continued to work as an electrician (as I had throughout college), and continued to feel the tug of philosophy. This tug was strong enough that I started going to night school to learn Greek, the language of philosophy, and eventually found my way to the University of Chicago. My studies there were interrupted by a stint in a cubicle job that I will describe later, but ultimately I earned a Ph.D. in the history of political thought. I then managed to stay on with a one-year gig at the university's Committee on Social Thought, on the third floor of Foster Hall.

The office next to mine on one side belonged to the South African novelist J. M. Coetzee; on the other side was the classicist David Grene, who seemed to be an immortal ancient himself (he was in his nineties). It was good company, if a bit intimidating, and I had been incredulously grateful to get the appointment. During this year I was supposed to be turning my dissertation into a book and applying for teaching jobs. But trying to make my dissertation fit into the standard forms of academic publishing was something I despaired of being able to pull off. Related to that, the academic job market was utterly depressing. I sent off some job applications in which I took pains to carefully frame my academic work in its intellectual context, and the only response I got was a series of postcards, which I was to return after checking some boxes specifying my race, gender, and sexual orientation. Stepping outside the intellectually serious circle of my teachers and friends at Chicago into the broader academic world, it struck me as an industry hostile to thinking. I once attended a conference entitled "After the Beautiful." The premise was a variation on "the death of God," the supposed disenchantment of the world, and so forth. Speaking up for my own sense of enchantment, I pointed out, from the audience, the existence of beautiful human bodies. Youthful ones, in particular. This must have touched a nerve, as it was greeted with incredulous howls of outrage from some of the more senior harpies.

So, for a number of reasons, I failed to develop a sincere aspiration to be a professor. The responsible thing would have been to figure out, quickly, how I was going to make a living come June. But my response was more like denial: I retreated to a makeshift workshop I set up in the basement of a Hyde Park apartment building, tearing down a 1975 Honda CB360 and rebuilding it as a café racer. The physicality of it, and the clear specificity of what the project required of me, was a balm for feelings of professional panic. Each morning that winter I would arrive with a hammer and a large screwdriver, and proceed to the day's first task: chipping my way through the ice that encased the gate that led down to the basement. A spectacular ice cliff, like a frozen waterfall, had formed over the entire rear fire escape early in the winter. Each day enough of it melted, then refroze at night, so the gate could be freed only by hammer and chisel. Inside the gate and down a short flight of stairs, I kept a basin of solvent stashed under the stairway; this was the parts-cleaning area. It doubled as the refrigerator. I had an unspoken understanding with the resident janitor, Dwayne, based on my inexact accounting for the beer I kept under the stairway and his failure to notice the open container of highly inflammable solvent, next to the beer. Through another door was the shop proper, which I had made pretty comfortable by tapping into the common, unmetered electrical panel for lights and power. An air compressor was made possible by the generous support of the John M. Olin Foundation (they thought their money was going toward a book on Plutarch). The compressor provided power to drive pneumatic tools: a die grinder, an impact wrench, a cutoff wheel. Heat was never a problem, due to the presence of a manifold for the building's boiler. The boiler itself was in another basement, which was ideal. Not only did this spare me the noise, it also made welding and grinding a less anxious affair, as the only explosive vapors present were those I generated myself. It was easy enough to keep the sparks and open flames away from things I could see: the electrical contact cleaner, carburetor cleaner, engine degreaser, cutting oil (one for ferrous metals, another for aluminum), moly grease, lithium grease, gasoline, antiseize compound, oxygen tank, acetylene tank, and whatnot. It was my own environmental holocaust, stewing away beneath the very domiciles of unsuspecting academics.

I hadn't really intended this. What started as a carburetor rebuild had gotten out of hand; I kept pulling things off the bike until I was down to a bare frame, and my fellowship checks were going mostly toward tools. It felt like I'd picked up right where I'd left off in my teenage education as a gearhead, and the intervening studies of ancient Greek began to feel like a parallel dream life.

Stumped by a starter motor that seemed to check out in every way (it had the specified impedance through its windings, and turned freely in its bearings) but wouldn't work, I started asking around at Honda dealerships. Nobody had an answer; finally one service manager told me to call Fred Cousins of Triple "O" Service. "If anyone can help you, Fred can."

The Motorcycle Antiquarian

I called Fred, and he invited me to come to his shop on Goose Island. This is an island on the Chicago River, just west of the Loop. It is an industrial wasteland, eerily quiet and desolate. As I would learn later from Fred's Snap-on dealer, who had serviced the area for over twenty years, the building next to Fred's was a rendering plant where animal parts were reduced to glue. The dealer claimed to have firsthand knowledge that the local mob used the place to dispose of human bodies with some regularity. A big car would back up to the loading bay and the workers at the plant would be told to take a long break.

I followed Fred's directions to an unmarked door on a blank-looking warehouse. He opened the door with a hard and somewhat skeptical look on his face, then instantly softened when he saw the starter motor in my hands. We climbed the stairs to the second floor, which was all his, then entered a space that had been partitioned off from the rest of the warehouse. There were two lifts; each held a Ducati at eye level. Crowded around the shop were Aermacchis, MV Augustas, Benellis, and some other Italian makes I had never even heard of, as well as quite a few Hondas from the 1960s and '70s. They were bathed in the slanting light of a Chicago winter in late afternoon; one wall of the shop was solid windows from waist level up.

Fred told me to put the motor on a certain bench that was free of clutter. He checked the impedance, as I had done, to confirm there was no short circuit or discontinuity. He spun the shaft in its bearings, as I had. He hooked it up to a battery. It moved ever so slightly, but wouldn't spin. Then he grabbed the shaft and tried to wiggle it side to side. "Too much free play." He suggested the problem was the bushing that located the end of the shaft in the motor housing—it was worn. When a current is applied to the windings, it produces not only a torque but also an initial sideways force. Free to move too much (perhaps a few hundredths of an inch), the rotor was binding on the motor housing. Fred scrounged around for a Honda motor. He found one with the same bushing, then used a "blind hole bearing puller" to extract it, as well as the one in my motor. Then he gently tapped the new, or rather newer, one into place. The motor worked. Then Fred gave me a succinct dissertation on the peculiar metallurgy of these Honda starter motor bushings of the mid-seventies. Here was a scholar.

Over the next six months I spent a lot of time at Fred's shop, learning, and put in only occasional appearances at the Committee. His whole scene seemed too groovy to be real, and provided an example of a life that was enviable to me. It also got me thinking about possible livelihoods. As it happened, in the spring I got a call from a former teacher, now in Washington, D.C., asking if I was interested in a job as director of a certain think tank. The salary was huge. Hell, yes, I was interested. I interviewed, and ended up getting the job. But I would quickly discover it was not to my taste. It was concerned more with the forms of inquiry than with the substance; the trappings of scholarship were used to put a scientific cover on positions arrived at otherwise. These positions served various interests, ideological or material. For example, part of my job consisted of making arguments about global warming that just happened to coincide with the positions taken by the oil companies that funded the think tank. Fred's life seemed more liberal.

One of the earliest uses of the word "liberal" was to draw a distinction between the "liberal arts" and the "servile arts." The former were those pursuits befitting a free man, while the latter were identified with the mechanical arts. I landed the job at the think tank because I had a prestigious education in the liberal arts, yet the job itself felt illiberal: coming up with the best arguments money could buy. This wasn't work befitting a free man, and the tie I wore started to feel like the mark of the slave. As I sat in my K Street office, Fred's life as an independent tradesman gave me an image of liberality that I kept coming back to.

Shockoe Moto

After five months at the think tank I'd saved enough to buy some tools I needed, and quit. I was going to go into business fixing motorcycles. My plan was to start small, working out of my garage. But I soon met Tommy, who had a line on some warehouse space that could be had for cheap rent. We went in on it together; my share of the rent was a hundred dollars per month.

For the first three years of its existence, my shop was located in this brick warehouse, near the train station in the decaying downtown area of Richmond called Shockoe Bottom. The business grew fitfully during this time, with always-uncertain prospects in a leaking, uninsurable building that sat at ground zero of a planned baseball stadium. One day I surveyed the cans of gasoline, the solvent circulating in the parts cleaner, and above all the makeshift squatter's wiring, and decided it was time to move. And in fact, the building has since burned down. But the episode I want to relate shortly, involving a Honda Magna, took place in this warehouse, so allow me to describe the scene.

The warehouse held an underground economy, completely invisible from the street. In addition to my shop, known as Shockoe Moto to those who knew which glazed-over window to knock on, there was a two-man cabinet shop, and two other motorcycle mechanics operating independently. Down the hall was Garnet, the laconic Harley and Brit-bike old-timer with his Whitworth wrenches and long pauses, working in the gloom cast by a single drop light in the cavernous darkness. Sharing my well-lit space was Tommy, a painter of nudes and diagnoser of steering shimmies. Elsewhere in the building there was an "architectural salvage" (that is, junk) dealer rumored to deal other things as well; a building contractor with an unintelligible South Carolina accent who carried around a spinal tap of morphine for a broken back; another builder, this one a lesbian gut-and-rehab, crack-house turnaround hustler; the warehouse drunk, unpredictably loving or vicious, with his interminable Olds Toronado restoration project; a black duck named BD with a taste for ankle flesh; and The Iraqi and his silk-shirt-wearing brother, who together "managed" the building. There were also various litters of kittens and a rotating series of questionable individuals, usually "in between situations," living upstairs in the unheatable, uncoolable warehouse, including one very sexy young S and M model and a pizza delivery guy who shot a man in self-defense and then skipped town, leaving behind only a Koran and a pile of porn. I'd gone from the Committee on Social Thought to this.

The illicit character of the whole scene made me feel more at ease than I had ever felt at a job or an academic conference. Everybody was on the wrong side of propriety, at the very least. This matched my sense of my own place in the world. Going to work didn't require putting on a costume, literally or psychically. Also, the warehouse contained many decades' worth of abandoned detritus. You were forever discovering cool old stuff, whole miniature worlds, in rooms you didn't even know existed. This haphazard physical environment seemed better suited to inquiry than my sterile think tank office on K Street. The jumble of it supported a spirit of experimentation.

Once I was cleaning a wheel bearing in the solvent tank. After this step, you blow it dry using compressed air. Twenty years earlier, at the Porsche shop, I had been told never to let a bearing spin when drying it. But I hadn't been told why. Tommy was standing ten feet away. He said, "Don't let it spin." It turned out he didn't know why, either. At that point we both knew what was coming next. I directed the air tangentially to the bearing, and it started to spool up with a sound like a turbine. Tommy came closer. "Cool!" Garnet, the old-timer, happened to be walking by, and came in. "Hey, Garnet, you ever spin a bearing with air?" He smiled and said nothing. Now I cranked up the pressure on the compressor's regulator and held the air gun on the bearing for a good long while. The pitch of the spinning bearing continued to rise, to the point it sounded like a dentist's drill. Grinning over the bearing, Tommy and I turned to Garnet. But Garnet was gone. The next thing I knew, the bearing felt a lot lighter in my hand, and there was a terrible racket up in the beams of the ceiling, like we were under rifle fire. The bearing had exploded, and all that remained in my hand was the inner race. Tommy and I felt lucky to be alive, and more inclined to heed Garnet's inscrutable silences.

Writing Service Tickets

I keep a logbook in the shop, a sort of motorcycle diary that serves a number of purposes. It is a record of bikes taken in, work done, and lessons learned. Sometimes I draw pictures to help myself reason through some mechanical situation. I measure various tolerances, when rebuilding a clutch, for example, and list them next to the wear limits specified in the service manual, if I have one for the bike. I also record the amount of time I spend on each task, and the money I've spent on parts. The book serves as a rough draft, then, for the service ticket I eventually write for the customer. It is rough because I have to make a judgment about how much detail the owner is interested in, and also about how truthful it is prudent to be.

I record hours on the left side of the page. Under that number, I'll write another number, the hours I think I ought to bill.

5.5 R&R front end, rebuild forks.

Bill: 2.5

This entry means that I actually spent around five and a half hours removing and replacing the front end of a motorcycle, tearing down the forks and cleaning their parts, inspecting everything for cracks and wear, putting in new fork seals and crush washers (these are washers made of copper or aluminum, used for sealing bolt holes; the forks contain oil), and putting the whole mess together again. But more often than not, I will bill for much less time. This was especially so when I first started. Early on, I decided it was best to lie about how much time it took me to do things, because the time I was spending seemed implausible. Partly it is inexperience that slows me down, and partly it is my disposition to get totally absorbed in the details, and forget that the clock is ticking. Also, my market niche lies in the fact that I am one of few people who will work on just about anything, so it is often the case that I am seeing an uncommon motorcycle, for the first time, and have to learn my way around it. The dealerships sometimes refuse to work on old bikes because they are prone to complications, and may require a bit of improvisational engineering. Some of the manufacturers no longer exist. Finding parts can be an endless hassle. Such bikes become "projects," and the last thing a service manager wants to do is break the rhythm of his mechanics. They get to be very fast, these dealer mechanics, and as an independent mechanic I feel I have to meet the standards of efficiency that they set, or at least appear to. So I lie and tell people a job took ten hours when it might have taken twenty. To compensate, I also tell them my shop rate is forty dollars per hour, but it usually works out to more like twenty. I feel like an amateur, no less now than when I started, but through such devices I hope to appear like somebody who knows what he is doing, and bills accordingly.[1]

This gap between my private logbook and the service ticket is the space where the ethics of repairing motorcycles gets worked out. Especially when working on old bikes, in trying to solve an existing problem I'll sometimes create a new problem. For example, to remove the brass float needle seat on a Bing carburetor (used on BMWs), the prescribed method is to use a tap to thread it; then you can put a pair of vise grips on the tap and pull the seat out from its recess. Once I was doing this and the tap broke off inside the seat. What now? Now you consider drilling out the tap. But the broken end is jagged, so you can't really get a drill bit to stay on the center of it. How do you bill for time spent solving a problem of your own making? There is no obvious answer to this question. Self-recrimination and a despairing sense of responsibility compete with a more soothing option: invoke Fate. But even if I take the latter approach, the question remains: Whose bill of misfortune should this be added to, mine or the owner's? This question has to be answered when you write the service ticket.

Some mechanics, like Pirsig's idiot, seem to have not enough concern for the motorcycle. I have suggested this moral failure tends to coincide with the cognitive failure of getting anchored in snap diagnostic judgments, and not being sufficiently attentive to the bike. Further, that the challenge for such a mechanic is to get outside his own head. I would now like to explore a different problem (my own), that of being obsessive about a motorcycle, and consider how this, too, can be a matter of selfishness. Sometimes I drive the bill up because I'm servicing my own compulsion. There is often a strain between my concern for the bike and my fiduciary responsibility to the owner. The economic exchange between us introduces another layer to the work, then, a metacognition where the factual question of what the bike needs gets complicated by the existence of multiple perspectives.

Of Madness, a Magna, and Metaphysics

I once got a call from a guy with a 1983 Honda Magna V45. This is kind of an uninspiring bike, to my taste. Further, the thing had been sitting for two years. Such calls are fairly common, if you're known as someone willing to deal with old bikes, especially someone willing to pick them up. Inevitably, these conversations include an assertion that "it ran fine when I parked it." It took me a few years, and lots of head scratching over mechanical situations that, no matter how I tried, could not be attributed to sitting, to realize the basic implausibility of such recollections. If it had run fine then, it wouldn't have been sitting for the last two years.

But it was winter, and business was slow. Being of two minds about this job, I tried my best at the outset to scare the owner: "Assuming it's got all the usual problems from sitting, you're looking at a thousand dollars to get it back on the road. The carbs will need to be gone through, it'll need new fork seals, new battery, new tires, probably new hydraulic lines, and who knows what else, so a thousand is about the minimum." This bike had one of the early Honda V4 engines, and they had problems with excessive wear in the valve train. "Have you kept the valves adjusted?" He had no recollection of ever having the valves adjusted. "You might want to just get rid of it."

This speech was a preemptive assault to adjust the expectations of the owner. A slap in the face, speeches like this are intended to highlight the irrational character of an owner's attachment to his decrepit old motorcycle. The more experience I have acquired, the more ruthless I have become in making such speeches. But here I am caught in a contradiction, since my entire business model is based on precisely such irrational attachment. If the Magna owner did the sensible thing, I would have nothing to do.

It was some dim awareness of this fact that led me to imitate Fred. He would answer his phone with a high-pitched "Service!" I loved the generality of that greeting, and started doing the same at my shop. What is being serviced, exactly? Among other things, the psyches of people with irrational attachments to old motorcycles. Frank talk, even a little abuse, is part of the repertoire of every therapist. A guy wanders into my shop expecting some cozy bonding over the aesthetic pleasures of "vintage" motorcycles, and instead finds himself berated like a hapless neurotic caught onstage with Dr. Phil. Peel away the hopeful interpretations, and "vintage" stands revealed as simply "old."

The more breathing room I can get from the owner—the more I raise his expectations for the bill—the more discretion I have in dealing with the bike itself. When you are fixing bikes that are not worth the money it takes to get them running right, the tension I mentioned between your fiduciary responsibility to the bike owner and your metaphysical responsibility to the bike itself is especially acute. In retrospect, I now recognize the sign scrawled above the parts counter at Donsco ("Speed costs. How fast do you want to spend?") as an attempt to ease this stress, in the same way as my speech. It basically says, check your economic logic at the door or don't come in, because I can't answer to two masters. But, of course, no customer can simply disregard the larger frame of his or her economic life. Much as I would like to be responsible only to the motorcycle, I am responsible also to another person, with a limited budget.

Say the bike shows evidence of a substantial oil leak: a thick, three-dimensional layer of caked-on grime covers the bottom half of the engine and frame. It could be something easy to fix (a leaking oil tank, or an external oil line), or it could be something requiring a complete teardown of the motor (certain oil seals, for example). In the latter case, it's often best to write it off as a parts bike. But to make this determination, you have to first figure out where the oil is leaking from. The problem is that, once liberated from where it's supposed to be, oil flings everywhere in the blast of wind that comes with speed, so it's near impossible to say where the oil is leaking from unless you first get everything clean and dry, and cleaning the bike is a big job. You poke halfheartedly at it with a screwdriver, not quite accepting this sequence of tasks, and watch chunks of shit-colored bike cheese fall off onto the lift. Next come the rags, lots of them, and various caustic substances.

Once everything is spick-and-span, I'll sometimes spray all the suspect areas with athlete's foot powder spray. (The powder is white, and clings to surfaces, so oil leaks become more visible.) But before you can check for oil leaks, the bike needs to run. So you may need to spend a lot of time removing carburetors, disassembling and cleaning them, sorting out buggered wiring, and who knows what all, before you can fire the thing up. That is, before you can say whether it has a serious oil leak, which, if you had known at the outset, would have made the bike not worth putting all this effort into. So at the beginning of any resuscitation of an old bike, you try to think logically about a sequence of investigations and fixes that will reveal the most serious problems sooner rather than later.

The Magna was screwed every which way, including loose. Further, with gratuitous plastic covers here and there, and that swoopy eighties comfort bike look, it had about zero cool factor. There were probably millions of them rotting in junkyards around the world, and it seemed a bit mad that I was about to devote my precious time, and the customer's money, to sorting this one out. But I kind of needed the work. Thoughts of the bike's economic value receded as I wheeled it onto the lift. The warehouse was empty and silent. I could see my breath with each exhalation, dissolving quickly into the chill void. I stepped on a red lever, and a loud whoosh of compressed air raised the Magna up to eye level.

Based on what I'd read about valve train problems in this bike, I decided to check the valves first. The thing is, with the close fit of the frame, getting the valve cover off the rear bank of cylinders on this bike is like trying to get a ship out of a bottle. It just seems flatly impossible. You persist only because you know it must have been put on at some point in the past, and in theory every sequence of moves ought to be reversible. But if you're me, at least, eventually your mind starts to doubt even such unassailable logic, and you begin to entertain the idea of cutting the frame away and welding it back later. I get so focused on the problem at hand that, outside my tunnel vision, a wholesale insanity begins to sprout in support of my immediate goal.

I smelled something burning, and discovered my pants were on fire. I was standing too close to the propane heater, in between bouts of valve cover jujitsu. The cover was still stuck where it had been a few hours ago. At this point I'd exhausted my entire lexicon of "motherfucker"-based idioms, and was running perilously low on slurs against the Japanese. I was nearing a familiar point where I've descended through every level of madness and despair, and a certain calm takes over. I was reduced now to a more or less autistic repetition of valve cover manipulations I'd long ago determined to be futile, when suddenly the cover just fell out of its trap and lay free in my hand.

This is a common experience, actually, and in an effort to save time in assembling and disassembling things with an inscrutable Oriental fit to them, I used to try to hypnotize myself into a Zen-like state of resignation at the outset. It doesn't work, not for this Grasshopper. I have my own process, as they say. I call it the motherfucker process.

The cams and rockers looked fine. Beautiful, actually. All four valves on the number 2 cylinder were tight, so I adjusted them to spec: .005 in. By the time I got the valve covers back on, I was seven hours into the bike (this figure is truly embarrassing), with essentially zero progress toward getting it on the road. The tight valves wouldn't have prevented it from running well enough to get a fuller assessment of the bike. At my shop rate of forty dollars per hour, that would be two hundred eighty dollars, but there was no way I could charge him for seven hours. In any case, I now had less breathing room in dealing with the bike, as far as time and money spent. In retrospect, I should have left the valves alone and focused on stuff that was obviously a problem.

Like the carbs, for example. Getting them sorted required three trips across the river to Bob Eubank's motorcycle junkyard to scrounge for linkage, then a missing spring, then a carb body. But it is the clutch hydraulics I want to focus on in this story, as they show the moral tension I'd like to describe between a mechanic's metaphysical responsibility to the machine and his fiduciary responsibility to its owner.

The clutch wouldn't disengage. I bled the system but couldn't get all the air out of the lines. Air is compressible, so air in the system prevents the transmission of pressure through the hydraulic lines, which is necessary to move the heavy springs that sandwich the clutch together. So I rebuilt the master cylinder, which really means just disassembling it, cleaning it out thoroughly with solvent and compressed air, removing the glaze on the cylinder by scuffing it lightly with some gray Scotch-Brite, putting in a new piston and seal, and replacing some crush washers.

Still the system wouldn't bleed. So I removed the slave cylinder as well. The cavity where the slave cylinder mates with the engine case was full of nasty, emulsified goo. I noticed the seal

Clutch rod oil seal

on the back of the slave cylinder was badly deteriorated, and was glad to find the culprit; fluid was obviously leaking out of the slave. Once I'd cleaned all the goo out of the cavity, I noticed that an oil seal in the engine case immediately behind the slave cylinder looked kind of buggered. So I reasoned that the goo was actually a mixture of clutch fluid and motor oil; maybe oil leaking from the motor had caused the slave cylinder seal to deteriorate. Maybe they were different kinds of rubber, each able to withstand only one kind of fluid. I'd never heard any discussion of the issue. In any case, I wanted to replace that oil seal in the case. Like most oil seals, it was shaped like a doughnut. This one was about the size of a quarter. The inner diameter has a little lip that rubs against a rod, wiping oil from it as it moves back and forth through the seal. That rod moves when you squeeze the clutch lever.

But here caution was called for. Was the seal held simply by an interference fit in its hole in the engine case, or did it have a step in it that seated against a shoulder machined into the inner face of the case? Try as I might, I couldn't tell by shining my flashlight at it from every angle. In the first situation, the seal could be pulled from my vantage outside the bike, using a seal puller (or a carefully wielded screwdriver). In the second situation, replacing the seal could be done only from inside the motor. I could get more aggressive in trying to learn which situation I had by digging at the seal with a screwdriver, but this would damage it further.

I had a microfiche parts book for this bike, so I put the fiche into the old library reader that sits on my workbench, and killed the overhead fluorescent lights. I had to stop breathing as I peered into the reader, so that my breath wouldn't fog up the screen. The exploded diagram didn't answer my question. I was at an impasse, the kind where your limbs become heavy.

I lit a cigarette, and let the smoke form a screen between my eyes and the Magna. I became aware of the faint hum of the fluorescent fixtures, and the hour: it was late at night. I walked through the dark warehouse to the bathroom, where I discovered the water in the toilet had frozen solid. It occurred to me that the best business decision would be to forget I'd ever seen the ambiguously buggered oil seal. With a freshly rebuilt slave cylinder, the clutch worked fine. Even if my idle speculation about the weeping oil seal causing the failure of the slave cylinder seal was right, so what? It would take quite a while for the problem to reappear, and who knows if this guy would still own the bike by then. If it is not likely to be his problem, I shouldn't make it my problem.

But as I walked back into the fluorescent brightness of the shop, I wasn't thinking about the owner, only about the bike. I just couldn't let that oil seal go. The compulsion was setting in, and I did little to resist it. I started digging at the seal, my peripheral vision narrowing. At first I told myself it was exploratory digging. But the seal was suffering from my screwdriver, and at some point I had to drop the forensic pretense. I was going to get that little fucker out.

There is something perverse at work here, and I would like to understand it. That oil seal was the opening to Pandora's box: I felt compelled to get to the bottom of things, to gape them open and clean them out. But this lust for thoroughness is at odds with the world of human concerns in which the bike is situated, where all that matters is that the bike works. The bike is for riding, and riding motorcycles competes for resources with other purposes the owner surely has. This more holistic, pragmatic view of the motorcycle is the one where economics becomes salient. It grounds the fiduciary responsibility of the mechanic to the owner. In digging at that oil seal heedlessly, I was acting out of some need of my own. The curious man is always a fornicator, according to Saint Augustine. In this case, it was the owner of the bike who would get fornicated, when I handed him the bill.

One theologian writes that "curiosity's desire is closed, limited by the object it wants to know considered in isolation: the knowledge curiosity seeks is wanted as though it were the only thing to be had."[2] The problem with such fixation is that the mechanic's activity, properly understood, is *practical* in character, rather than curious or theoretical. As such it must be disciplined by a circumspect regard for others, a kind of fiduciary consciousness. Amy Gilbert writes that practical wisdom entails "the full appreciation of the salient moral features of the particular situations we confront. Our awareness of these features enables us to respond properly to them."[3] Acquiring practical wisdom, then, entails overcoming the self-absorption of the idiot, but also the tunnel vision of the curious man whose attention is indeed directed outside of himself, but who sees only his own goal. A lot of academic work has this quality of curiosity without circumspection; my own Ph.D. dissertation proceeded in a way similar to the Magna oil seal episode. But with the Magna I had to give an account to the customer.

The metaphysician often takes a dim view of economic exchange. It is the realm of mere agreement and conventional valuations, rather than intrinsic qualities. But agreement and convention, if consulted, provide a helpful check on your own subjectivity—they offer proof that you are not insane, or at least a more robust presumption to that effect. Some of us need such proof more than others, and getting paid for what you love to do can provide it. Going into business is good therapy for the feeling that there is something arbitrary and idiosyncratic in your grasp of the world, and therefore that your actions within it are unjustified.

The oil seal turned out to be one that, of course, could be replaced only from the inside—a huge job. I ended up pulling the final drive unit (the Magna is shaft-driven) and the swing arm to replace that oil seal. Doing so gave me great satisfaction. But like that of the fornicator, this pleasure brought a surge of bad conscience in its wake. In the end I knocked the labor bill from $2,200 down to $1,500. This entailed a belated recognition that the quality of being wide-awake, of being a clear-sighted person who looks around and sees the whole situation, isn't something I can take for granted in myself. It is something that needs to be achieved on a moment-to-moment basis. The presence of others in a shared world makes this both possible and necessary.

6

The Contradictions of the Cubicle

The popularity of *Dilbert, The Office,* and any number of other pop-culture windows on cubicle life attests to the dark absurdism with which many Americans have come to view their white-collar work. Absurdity is good for comedy, but bad as a way of life. It usually indicates that somewhere beneath the threshold of official notice fester contradictions that, if commonly admitted, would bring on some kind of crisis. What sort of contradictions might these be? To begin with, we are accustomed to think of the business world as ruled by an amoral bottom-line mentality, but in fact it is impossible to make sense of the office without noticing that it has become a place of moral education, where souls are formed and a particular ideal of what it means to be a good person is urged upon us.

This contradiction is perhaps rooted in a more basic one. Corporations portray themselves as results-based and performance-oriented. But where there isn't anything material being produced, objective standards for job performance are hard to come by. What is a manager to do? He is encouraged to direct his attention to the states of minds of workers, and become a sort of therapist.

By way of contrast, consider the relationship between a machinist and his shop boss. The machinist makes his part, then hands it to the boss. Let us imagine the boss pulls his micrometer out of his breast pocket, and either finds the part within spec or doesn't. If he doesn't, he looks at the worker with displeasure, or maybe curses him, because either he failed to read the drawing correctly, failed to clamp it properly in the machine, spaced out while cutting, or doesn't know how to use his own micrometer. Whatever the cause, the worker's failing is sitting on the bench, staring both parties in the face, and this object is likely to be the focal point of the conversation. But in the last thirty years American businesses have shifted their focus from the production of goods (now done elsewhere) to the projection of brands, that is, states of mind in the consumer, and this shift finds its correlate in the production of mentalities in workers. Process becomes more important than product, and is to be optimized through management techniques that work on a deeper level than the curses of a foreman. Further, though the demands made on workers are invariably justified in terms of their contribution to the bottom line, in fact such calculations are difficult to make; the chain of means-ends reasoning becomes opaque, and this opens the way for work to become a rather moralistic place. James Poulos writes that in the office, "mutual respect and enthusiasm [have] reached new levels of performed social intimacy."[1] Those whose job it is to select and adjust workers to the realities of work have taken notice; in 2005 the *Journal of Organizational Behavior* devoted an entire section to the growing debate within their ranks over emotional intelligence, or "EI," as they call it. In the contemporary office, the whole person is at issue, rather than a narrow set of competencies.

To judge from business books, the demands made on managers themselves penetrate the most deeply. Thus in *Team-building That Gets Results* we find an Alert! box that reads "Does your feedback on a particular situation have more to do with your own ego or being 'right'? Think it through first. If you find your own ego lurking behind the feedback, put it to the side. . . ."[2] Surveying the popular titles in a chain bookstore, it becomes clear that management books are a subcategory of self-help books, and that adopting them as one's guide may lead one into "an inquisitorial morass of motive and self-accountability," to borrow a phrase.[3] Throughout this literature one finds an imperative for the manager to *care*, and to sincerely hold forth to his subordinates the possibility of *personal transformation*. He is not so much a boss as a life coach.

The contemporary office requires the development of a self that is ready for teamwork, rooted in shared habits of flexibility rather than strong individual character. I will be drawing some comparisons between the office and the job site, the team and the crew. At issue in the contrast between office work and the manual trades is the idea of *individual responsibility*, tied to the presence or absence of objective standards.

Indexing and Abstracting

After a one-year master's degree program at the University of Chicago, I had to put philosophy on hold and go back to work (I would return a couple of years later to begin a Ph.D. program). Rather than go back to the electrical work I'd done after college, I wanted to put my new degree to use and claim my place in the sunny uplands of the meritocracy. This turned out to be more difficult than I had anticipated. I landed a job as a clerk at a prestigious Palo Alto law firm, but the job paid only ten dollars an hour. So I worked there from eight to five, then taught SAT prep classes (for fifteen dollars an hour) farther up the peninsula after work, and often tutored in Marin after that. I was driving about a hundred miles a day (in a 1966 Malibu) in a three-bridge loop around San Francisco Bay before returning exhausted each night to my sublet in Berkeley. Then I was let go from the law firm. Shortly after that, the SAT prep company went bankrupt (I never saw the thousand dollars in back pay they owed me). At this juncture it would have made sense to chuck the "meritocracy" and go back to doing electrical work, for much better pay, but somehow I wasn't able to see my situation clearly and take this step. I had a *master's degree*, goddamit.

In 1942, Joseph Schumpeter wrote that the expansion of higher education beyond labor market demand creates for white-collar workers "employment in substandard work or at wages below those of the better-paid manual workers." What's more, "it may create unemployability of a particularly disconcerting type. The man who has gone through college or university easily becomes psychically unemployable in manual occupations without necessarily acquiring employability in, say, professional work."[4]

My self-regard as a Master of Arts was hard to sustain through the extended trauma of job hunting, with its desperate open-mindedness and rising sense of worthlessness. Finally I landed a job as an indexer and abstractor at Information Access Company, then a division of Ziff Communications, and stayed there for eleven months. I was excited about my first day on the job as I crested the high point of the San Mateo Bridge at 8:15 one bright morning in 1992, on a day windy enough to whitecap even the South Bay. My new job was to read articles in academic journals, index them under established categories, and write abstracts of about two hundred words, which were then sold on a CD-ROM to subscribing libraries, where they could be viewed on a system called InfoTrac. I was to be a knowledge worker. Indeed, here was an opportunity to survey the frontiers of knowledge and gain a synoptic view of the whole, which seemed in keeping with my academic preparation. What met my gaze more immediately, at that high point in my first commute, was the downslope into Foster City.

Foster City is a four-square-mile spit of landfill, a chunk of San Francisco Bay (once salt marsh tideland) that was essentially annexed by Silicon Valley in a kind of privateer action led by one T. Jack Foster to create a planned community for the post-industrial age. Anchoring the west end of the San Mateo Bridge, it was developed under a uniform aesthetic of business parks, marinas, and town houses that seem to share a common genetic code when viewed en masse from the apex of the bridge.

In the weeks between my interview and my first day on the job, the managers I had met had taken up residence in my imagination, where I often surprised them with my hidden depths. Such imaginings eased my sense of isolation and indeterminacy, which had begun to make me feel almost unreal. When I got the phone call offering me the job, I felt I had grabbed hold of the passing world—miraculously, through the mere filament of a classified ad—and reeled myself into its current. As I was shown to my cubicle by these same people, I felt a real sense of being honored. They had made a place for me. It seemed more than spacious enough. It was *my* desk, where I would think my thoughts, and no longer as a private amusement tending toward alienation. Rather, these thoughts would be my unique contribution to a common enterprise, in a real company with hundreds of employees. The regularity of the cubicles made me feel I had found a place in the order of things; I felt enlarged by the largeness of it. I would wear a tie.

But the feel of the job changed as I settled into it, and to understand the shift it is necessary to say how the job was conceived and structured. Information Access Company's (IAC) first product, in 1977, was Magazine Index, an index of about four hundred popular magazines. In 1980, IAC was acquired by Ziff, a publisher of magazines, and five years later Ziff merged IAC with another acquisition, Management Contents. Management Contents provided not only indexing but also abstracts of articles in management journals. So the introduction of abstracting to the company's activities coincided with the introduction of serious-looking journals, with all the trappings of scholarship. I suspect the leap from indexing to abstracting, and from magazines to journals, went smoothly, indeed appeared as no leap at all, because of the peculiar content of management journals. Articles in management journals typically contain about one idea for every five bullet points, so writing an abstract for one is as easy as stringing together every fifth bullet point. But in 1991, shortly before I started, the company began providing abstracts of articles in a very different class of journals: titles in physical science, biological science, social science, law, philosophy, and the humanities. The difference between, for example, *Marketing Today* and *Nature Genetics* (one of the titles I was assigned) is categorical, yet distinctions of rigor have a hard time withstanding immersion in the solvent of mergers and acquisitions that would reduce knowledge to "information."[5] Here is an excerpt from the "Letters" section of the current issue of *Nature Genetics* (as I write this in 2007):

> *We show that* miR-214 *is expressed during early segmentation stages in somites and that varying its expression alters the expression of genes regulated by Hedgehog signaling. Inhibition of* miR-214 *results in a reduction or loss of slow-muscle cell types. We show that* su(fu) *mRNA, encoding a negative regulator of Hedgehog signaling, is targeted by* miR-214.

In some journals, including *Nature Genetics*, articles begin with an abstract written by the author, but even in such cases I was to write my own. Nor was I simply to reword the author's abstract, as I learned in my initial week of training. Rather, I was to read the entire article and distill it afresh. The rationale offered was that unless I did so, there would be no "value added" by IAC's product. It was hard to believe I was going to add anything other than error and confusion to such material. But then, I hadn't yet been trained.

My job was structured on the supposition that in writing an abstract there is a method that merely needs to be applied, and that this does not require understanding (like a computer that manipulates syntax while remaining innocent of semantics). I was actually told this by the trainer, Monica, as she stood before a whiteboard diagramming an abstract. The writing of abstracts had been conceived in general terms, but I soon discovered that what the task in fact demanded was complete immersion in the particular text before me.[6] Monica seemed a perfectly sensible person, and gave no outward signs of suffering delusions. She didn't insist too much on what she was telling us, and it became clear she was in a position similar to that of a veteran Soviet bureaucrat who must work on two levels at once: reality and official ideology.

My starting quota, after finishing a week of training, was fifteen articles per day. By my eleventh month at the company, my quota was up to twenty-eight articles per day (this was the normal, scheduled acceleration). Whereas Charlie Chaplin's efforts to conform himself to the accelerating pace of the machine in *Modern Times* took the form of a brilliantly comic ballet, mine were rather mopey and anxious. More than anything, I felt sleepy. This exhaustion was surely tied to the fact I felt trapped in a contradiction.[7] The fast pace demanded absorption in the task, yet that pace also precluded absorption, and had the effect of estranging me from my own doings. Or rather, I *tried* to absent myself, the better to meet my quota, but the writing of an abstract, unlike the pulling of levers on an assembly line, cannot be done mindlessly. The material I was reading was too demanding, and what it demanded was to be given its due. To not do justice to an author who had poured his life into the subject at hand felt like violence against what was best in myself.

My efforts to read, comprehend, and write abstracts of twenty-eight academic journal articles per day required me to actively suppress my own ability to think, because the more you think, the more the inadequacies in your understanding of an author's argument come into focus. This can only slow you down. The quota demanded that I suppress as well my sense of responsibility to others—not just the author of an article but also the hapless users of InfoTrac, who might naïvely suppose that my abstract reflects the contents of that article. So the job required both dumbing down and a bit of moral reeducation.

Now, it is probably true that every job entails some kind of mutilation. Working as an electrician, you breathe a lot of unknown dust in crawl spaces, your knees get bruised, your neck gets strained from looking up at the ceiling while installing lights or ceiling fans, and you get shocked regularly, sometimes while on a ladder. Your hands are sliced up from twisting wires together, handling junction boxes made out of stamped sheet metal, and cutting metal conduit with a hacksaw. But none of this damage touches the best part of yourself.

It will be objected: Wasn't there any quality control? My manager would periodically read a few of my abstracts, and I was once or twice corrected and told not to begin an abstract with a dependent clause. But I was never confronted with an abstract I had written and told that it did not adequately reflect the article. The quality standards were the generic ones of grammar, internal to the abstract, which could be applied without my supervisor having to read the article. In this sense, I was not held to an external, objective standard.

It will further be objected that if the abstracts produced by Information Access Company were no good, then "the market" would punish it; the company should have been beaten out by one with a higher regard for quality. The company has been bought and sold several times since I worked there, but appears to still be in business. Maybe things are better there now, and quality has improved. I honestly don't know. In any case, the time scale on which the market administers its omniscient justice may be quite a bit longer than crucial episodes in the working life of a mortal human being. Being an early entrant into the market for electronically distributed abstracts, IAC enjoyed a temporary quasi-monopoly. I suppose it was fairly free to set standards as it pleased, and may have calibrated the production quota, and corresponding quality, to some threshold of "good enough," beneath which the user walks away in disgust.[8] Recurring purchases, after all, may continue even when the alignment of interests between producer and consumer is only partial, or even accompanied by a felt antagonism. Frequently we come to hate things that we nonetheless continue to depend on (like Windows). Further, a product made under conditions of harried intellectual carelessness, such as InfoTrac circa 1992, may generate its own demand by corrupting our standards in the same direction, and our initial harsh judgment of it will come to seem reactionary. The very existence of the product makes the lower standards suddenly seem respectable or inevitable.

In writing abstracts of academic journal articles, I thought I would learn a lot. Quite apart from the pay, the job seemed to promise an intrinsic good to me as a worker: satisfying my desire to know. This satisfaction is in perfect harmony with the good of the *user* of InfoTrac, who also desires to know, and the good of the author of an article, who wants to be understood. The standard internal to the job, properly conceived, was the very one that presumably animated both parties I served: intellectual excellence. But this good was nowhere accommodated by the metric to which I answered, which was purely quantitative. The metric was conceived by another party to the labor process, a middleman hovering about with a purpose of his own that had no inherent tie to the one shared by the principals. This purpose, of course, was that of realizing a profit from my labor.

As I have said elsewhere in this book, work is necessarily toilsome and serves someone else's interest. That's why you get paid. But, again, if I had been serving the user of the database directly, his interest in high-quality abstracts would have aligned with my own interest in experiencing the pleasures of comprehension. It may or may not be the case that selling my labor directly to the user would have given him a high-quality product at an attractive price *and* have provided me a comfortable livelihood; one would have to calculate whether such a transaction makes sense or not. And let it not be forgotten that my work would need to be marketed and distributed, as IAC did, and its technical bugs worked out, and this would contribute to the cost. Let it further be conceded that I never would have undertaken to launch such a product as InfoTrac on my own, and that the entrepreneurs who did so took risks. I have no beef with them. They made something, then sold it to others (the media conglomerate Ziff) who seem to be in the business of owning things. What I want to emphasize is that the presence of this third party seeking to *maximize* a surplus skimmed from my labor, in a manner not sensitive to the limitations of pace arising from the nature of the work itself, *must* drive the work process beyond those limits. It is then all but guaranteed that the work *cannot* be animated by the goods that are intrinsic to it. It is these intrinsic goods of the work that make me want to do it well. They closely track the "quality" of the product, that aspect that proves such an elusive metaphysical concept to those who merely count their surplus but which is a central and concrete concern for both the maker and the user of the thing itself.

Yet to identify greed as the problem would be to place the issue beyond serious address, leaving only impotent lamentation or a tedious exhortation to altruism. While greed may indeed be the root cause of our impoverished work life, it is surely not the case that the managers who design and orchestrate the work process are themselves greedy (or rather, they surely *are* greedy, no less or more than the rest of us, but that is not the issue). They are wage earners, and as likely as anyone else to hold themselves to a high ethical standard in their private lives. The problem, rather, is in the organization of managerial work within which they must operate.

Learned Irresponsibility

Managers are placed in the middle of an enduring social conflict that once gave rise to street riots but is mostly silent in our times: the antagonism between labor and capital. In this position they are subject to unique hazards. The sociologist Robert Jackall spent years inhabiting their world, conducting interviews, and describes its "peculiarly chancy and fluid" character. He shows the vulnerability of managers in their careers, and how it gives rise to a certain kind of language that they use, a highly provisional way of speaking and feeling. I believe some of the contradictions of "knowledge work" such as I experienced at Information Access Company can be traced to an imperative of abstraction, and that this imperative in turn may be understood as a device that upper-level managers use, quite understandably, to cope with the psychic demands of their own jobs.

To begin with, Jackall finds that though the modern workplace is in many respects a bureaucracy, managers do not experience authority in an impersonal way. Rather, authority is embodied in the persons with whom one has working relationships up and down the hierarchy. One's career depends entirely on these personal relationships, in part because the criteria of evaluation are ambiguous. As a result, managers have to spend a good part of the day "managing what other people think of them." With a sense of being on probation that never ends, managers feel "constantly vulnerable and anxious, acutely aware of the likelihood at any time of an organizational upheaval which could overturn their plans and possibly damage their careers fatally," as Craig Calhoun writes in his review of Jackall's book.[9] It is a "prospect of more or less arbitrary disaster."

A good part of the job, then, consists of "a constant interpretation and reinterpretation of events that constructs a reality in which it is difficult to pin blame on anyone, especially oneself," according to Calhoun. This gives rise to the art of talking in circles. Mutually contradictory statements are made to cohere by sheer forcefulness of presentation, allowing a manager to "stake out a position on every side of an issue. Or one buries what one wants done in a string of vaguely related descriptive sentences that demand textual exegesis," as Jackall writes.[10] The intent of this kind of language is not to deceive, it is to preserve one's interpretive latitude so that if the context changes, "a new, more appropriate meaning can be attached to the language already used. In this sense the corporation is a place where people are not held to what they say because it is generally understood that their word is always provisional."[11] Nothing is set in concrete the way it typically is when you are, for example, pouring concrete.

Managers may speak very colorfully with one another, for example, when describing their weekends, or even in reference to some situation at work, but such earthy talk takes place in a parallel universe of the private. In any group setting, they have to protect their bosses' "deniability" by using empty or abstract language to cover over problems, thereby keeping the field of subsequent interpretations as wide open as possible. "[T]he more troublesome a problem, the more desiccated and vague the public language describing it should be," according to Jackall.[12]

It is in this two-tiered system of language—direct in private, empty in public—that the world of managers resembles that of Soviet bureaucrats, who had to negotiate reality without public recourse to language that could capture it, obliged to use instead language the whole point of which was to cover over reality.

When a manager's success is predicated on the manipulation of language, for the sake of avoiding responsibility, reward and blame come untethered from good faith effort. He may then come to think that those beneath him in the food chain also can't be held responsible in any but arbitrary ways. One of the features commonly observed in ancient Near Eastern courts was that eunuchs were most capricious toward other eunuchs, those further from the center of power. The prerogative of doing so was part of the compensation package, so to speak.

One might be tempted to think this is demoralizing for all involved. But we are highly adaptive creatures, and these circumstances generate their own sort of morality, one in which the fixed points of an internal moral compass must give way to a certain sensitivity and nimbleness. Managers may continue to have strong convictions, but they are obliged to check them at the door, and expect others to do the same. "[M]oral viewpoints threaten others within an organization by making claims on them that might impede their ability to read the drift of social situations."[13] As a result there is social pressure (one might say a moral demand) not to be too "moralistic." This pressure is rooted in the insecurity of managerial careers.

My supervisor, Carol, was herself a writer of abstracts, which made her situation as enforcer of the quota poignant. As an abstractor, she doubtless felt trapped in the same contradiction as I. She was a bookish person, so I imagine she had some love for intellectual precision. But this was likely an "inappropriate" value to bring to the table when pleading the case of abstractors before her bosses (which I like to imagine she did). Such concerns can be rendered appropriate, and higher-level management support secured, only by demonstrating how they contribute to profits. Not because the higher-level managers are heartless, but because such a demonstration provides everyone needed cover. In fact, a lower-level manager may need only to put on a *performance* of hardheadedness before her superiors, and produce the stage props of a profit-maximizing calculation (graphs, charts, and so on). Unless she has these skills of the corporate dramatist, she is unlikely to get the official cover she needs to do the right thing by her workers.

Given the moral maze inhabited by managers, we can understand why those higher in the hierarchy must absent themselves from the details of the production process: such abstraction facilitates nonaccountability. Lower-level managers can't help but think concretely, and their proximity to the work process makes them aware also of its human character, including the damage it does. This was Carol's situation, that of being caught in the middle. The damage in question includes not only such problems as carpal tunnel syndrome, but the self-estrangement that arises from a work pace that ruthlessly subordinates the intrinsic goods of the job to the extrinsic metric of profit.

At lunchtime I had a standing arrangement with two other abstractors. One was from my group, a laconic, disheveled man named Mike, whom I liked instantly. He did about as well on his quota as I did on mine (which was not very well), but it didn't seem to bother him too much. The other guy was from beyond the partition, a meticulously groomed Liberian named Henry, who had worked for the CIA in his country. He had had to flee Liberia very suddenly one day, and soon found himself resettled near the office parks of Foster City. Henry wasn't going to sweat the quota. Come twelve thirty the three of us would hike overland, as it were, to the food court in the mall. It would be hard to overstate the sense of release that came with this movement. It involved traversing several "campuses," with ponds frequented by oddly real seagulls, then the lunch itself, which I always savored. This calls to mind Marx, who writes that under conditions of estranged labor, man "no longer feels himself to be freely active in any but his animal functions." Over lunch Mike would recount the outrageous things he had written in his abstracts, which were then published under the names of untenured assistant professors. I could see my own future in such furtive moments of sabotage—the compensating pleasures of a cubicle drone. Always funny and gentle, one day Mike confided that he was doing quite a bit of heroin. On the job. This actually made some sense.

How was it that I, once a proudly self-employed electrician, had ended up among these walking wounded, a "knowledge worker" at a salary of $23,000? I hadn't gone to graduate school for the sake of a career (rather, I wanted guidance reading some difficult books), but once I had the master's degree I felt like I belonged to a certain order of society, and was entitled to its forms. Despite the beautiful ties I wore, it turned out to be a more proletarian existence than I had known as a manual worker.

Interlude: What College Is For

If I had pursued higher education for the sake of a career, it would have turned out to be a complete mistake; happily, this was not my situation, and I have no regrets about my studies. But many people seem to regard college, and even graduate school, as an extension of compulsory schooling. More than 90 percent of high school students "report that their guidance counselors encouraged them to go to college."[14]

In this there is little accommodation of the diversity of dispositions, and of the fact that some very smart people are totally ill suited both to higher education and to the kind of work you're supposed to do once you have a degree. Further, funneling everyone into college creates certain perversities in the labor market.

The sociologist of education Randall Collins describes a cycle of credential inflation that "could go on endlessly, until janitors need Ph.D.'s and babysitters are required to hold advanced degrees in child care."[15] The escalating demand for academic credentials gives the impression of an ever more knowledgeable society, whose members perform cognitive feats their unschooled parents could scarcely conceive of. Consider my abstracting job as it might have been described by a business journalist steeped in the latest talk about a "postindustrial society" or "creative economy." I perfectly exemplified the knowledge worker, and what's more, I had an advanced degree to match. My very existence, multiplied a millionfold, is precisely what puts the futurologist in a rapture: we are getting to be so smart! Yet, in viewing my situation from afar in this way, the M.A. degree serves only to obscure a more real stupidification of the work I secured with that credential, and a wage to match. What the hell is going on? Is this our society as a whole, buying more education only to scale new heights of stupidity?

If much corporate knowledge work is after all not terribly demanding on the brain, or even requires the active suppression of intelligence, then we would expect academic accomplishments to be a poor basis on which to make hiring decisions. And in fact, corporate recruiters say they care little about a student's grades. The university itself is trusted to have done more than enough cognitive sorting on the day it admitted a student. In their book *Higher Education and Corporate Realities*, the sociologists Phillip Brown and Richard Scase quote one recruiter saying, "We find no correlation at all between your degree result and how well you get on in this company. Not at all. I wish there were. I would then be able to say, 'Unless you've got [a good GPA], don't bother.'"[16]

The irrelevance of what you actually learn (or don't) in school for job performance is hard to square with a technocratic view of the economy, which is invariably coupled with a sunny presumption of meritocracy. Together, these views sometimes go by the name of "human capital theory." According to this theory, "schools help society get the skills that it needs while they help individuals get the social positions that they deserve," as David Labaree put it in *How to Succeed in School Without Really Learning: The Credential Race in American Education.*[17]

This technocratic/meritocratic view strikes us today as common sense, but it is predicated on a certain view of what education is for, one that arose in the last century. In the years after World War II, many observers were struck with how complex society was becoming. The rational and scientific administration of this complexity seemed imperative; mere common sense seemed a paltry thing, totally inadequate to the challenges of a modern economy. Many business executives who were doing the hiring in the postwar years lacked degrees themselves, and assumed that college graduates would make superior employees because they possessed super-duper skills and knowledge. They were eager to hire college graduates to do jobs that had long been done by people with only high school diplomas. Yet there was little evidence to show they were better at their jobs, and in many cases they were less so. In a famous study of air traffic controllers, a job requiring complex decision making, for example, the sociologist Ivar Berg found an inverse correlation between educational achievement and job performance.[18]

Further, the technocratic/meritocratic view of education treats it as instrumental—it is good for society, and for getting ahead—and this has a corrupting effect on genuine education. As Labaree writes, "Formal characteristics of schooling—such as grades, credits, and degrees—come to assume greater weight than substantive characteristics, as pursuing these badges of merit becomes more important than actually learning anything along the way. . . . Teaching takes a back seat to the more socially salient task of sorting, and grading becomes more important for its social consequences than for its pedagogical uses."[19]

Pedagogically, you might want to impress on a student the miserable state of his mind. You might want to improve the student by first crushing him, as then you can recruit his pride to the love of learning. You might want to reveal to him the chasm separating his level of understanding from the thinkers of the ages. You do this not out of malice, but because you sense rare possibilities in him, and take your task to be that of cultivating in the young man (or woman) a taste for the most difficult studies. Such studies are likely to embolden him against timid conventionality, and humble him against the self-satisfaction of the age, which he wears on his face. These are the pedagogical uses of the "D." But give someone a low grade, and he is likely to press upon you the fact that his admission to law school hangs in the balance. The Sort is on.

With this attitude, students are merely adapting themselves to the marketlike ethic of the institutions that school them. As Labore writes, "Educational institutions find themselves located in a hierarchy of their own, forced to compete with other institutions for position in order to enhance the marketability of their credentials to socially mobile consumers."[20] The result is "a growing emphasis on producing selective symbolic distinctions rather than shared substantive accomplishments."[21] That is, what matters is your rank among your peers; it matters not if the whole lot of you are ignorant. When the point of education becomes the production of credentials rather than the cultivation of knowledge, it forfeits the motive recognized by Aristotle: "All human beings by nature desire to know." Students become intellectually disengaged.

Maybe we *can* say, after all, that higher education is indispensable to prepare students for the jobs of the information economy. Not for the usual reason given, namely, that there is ever-increasing demand for workers with more powerful minds, but in this perverse sense: college habituates young people to accept as the normal course of things a mismatch between form and content, official representations and reality. This cannot be called cynicism if it is indispensable to survival in the contemporary office, as it was in the old Soviet Union.

Thirty years ago, Collins pointed out that higher education serves a signaling function: it rewards and certifies the display of middle-class self-discipline. But what sort of discipline is required of white-collar workers these days? Once upon a time, the passing of examinations, meeting of course deadlines, and disciplined study for the sake of mastering a body of knowledge broadcast a willingness to conform to organizational discipline, and displayed the dispositions needed to develop competence in a bureaucracy. But the new antibureaucratic ideal of the *flexible* organization puts quite different demands on people, requiring the cultivation of a different sort of self. As Brown and Scase point out, in the new dispensation the whole person is at issue; one has to have certain personal qualities, more than a well-defined set of competencies tied to the fulfillment of specific organizational ends. What the recruiters are looking for is a manner of personal comportment, a collection of psychological and social aptitudes, that is difficult to codify. (This makes sense for a workplace that has little in the way of objective standards such as one finds in a machine shop.) Accordingly, the credentialism of higher education can continue its signaling function only if the official items appearing on a transcript are supplemented with extracurricular items that signal the possession of a complete personality *package*.[22] Students and their parents seem to understand this. An important part of the package is that one be a joiner, as this signals the possession of a self that is ready for "teamwork."

Teamwork

The rise of teamwork coincides with the discovery of "corporate culture" by management theorists in the late 1970s. The term was no longer meant as a sneering condemnation of the man in the gray flannel suit, but as a new realm of possibility. David Franz writes that "the expectation that corporate culture could be *managed* was both central to its appeal and its crucial conceptual innovation."[23] The idea that culture can be managed entails a reversal of the usual idea of culture. "Culture, as social scientists use the term, is a mostly subterranean force, taken for granted, assumed, inarticulate. We are born into cultures, which teach us how to see, speak, and think. It is only through great effort that we can bring our own culture into view and then only partially. Corporate cultures, however, can be diagnosed, evaluated, and altered."[24] Managers needed to become anthropologists. But above all they needed to become *founders* of cultures, like a Moses, Jesus, or Muhammad. That is, their anthropological finesse would not take the form of detached analysis, but rather of charismatic world making (with executive pay to match). The discovery of corporate culture opened the way for new and uncanny modes of manipulation in the office.

Through the exercise of charismatic authority, the manager *unsettles* others, shaking them out of their cramped views and stale habits, thereby unleashing the creativity of all workers. This is a charismatic leader of a new kind, a sort of radical democrat. He does not seek followers; he seeks to make every man a leader of himself. Authority itself disappears as he turns work into play. He erects Nerf basketball hoops; he announces pajama day. The creative class expands.

Such innovations arose in Silicon Valley, the epicenter of hopes for the transformation of work through technology. In 1966, Philip Rieff wrote that the ideal character type of the coming age will be "a man of leisure, released by technology from the regimental discipline of work so as to secure his well-being in highly refined alloplastic ways."[25] It would not have surprised Rieff that "leisure" can become "play," and then absorbed into work. The self overflows the "regimental discipline of work," but such overflowing may take the form of longer hours in the office.

Workers must *identify* with the corporate culture, and exhibit a high level of "buy-in" to "the mission." The division between private life and work life is eroded, and accordingly the whole person is at issue in job performance evaluations. This exposure may be on all sides; some managers are now subject to the "360 review," in which they answer not to a superior alone (the hierarchy has been smashed), but to all of their coworkers, and indeed to the assessments of customers and suppliers. Such reviews resemble the "encounter group" therapy sessions of the 1970s, in which one person was placed in the "hot seat" and then berated from every side. The point was to break down the ego, cleansing it of those false self-conceptions we call our "identity." Thus purified, the ego can be built up once again by the group through praise. In *Teambuilding That Gets Results*, we find this:

> *Team Activity: Building Egos for Team Strength. Each team member's name is written on a piece of paper, which is then folded and put in a basket. Each member pulls a name from the basket and takes one minute to write down as many positive attributes for that person as possible. When this is done, each person in the group identifies the person they picked and articulates his or her praise verbally. Before moving on to the next team member, the person receiving the feedback is asked, "Is that how you view yourself? Please explain."*[26]

The purpose of the activity is to "accentuate the positive" and build self-esteem. But this is self-esteem of a particular sort, refracted through the assessments of the Team. It is perhaps not so much "building egos" as reconstituting the ego, so that the Team becomes the controlling unit of personality. There are further devices that can be used for breaking down the individual. Elsewhere in *Teambuilding That Gets Results*,[27] we get an example of such an exercise. Six to ten people are assembled and given a light wooden dowel. Their objective is to lower it to the ground, together, after it has been placed horizontally on their outstretched fingers. What happens is that, contrary to each individual's will, the dowel goes up rather than down. "Surprise and great laughter ensue." The facilitator offers them reminders of the difference between up and down. "That's the floor. That's the ceiling. Slipping off the dowel makes the group start again from the beginning—which builds more frustration." This frustration is a key part of the pedagogy. As the would-be team continues to fail at their appointed task, she gently berates them. "I tell them that this is a very light wooden dowel—you just need to lower it together to the floor." Each time she starts them over she puts downward pressure on the dowel. That is, she gives them the impression the dowel is heavier than it is, so they begin by putting more upward pressure on the dowel than they would if they sensed its true weight, which dooms them to their theater of failure. This failure would seem to be based on the assumption that the facilitator is acting in good faith. Eventually "the group begins to anticipate this, and they start to prepare each other for it." What then? Having shed their false consciousness and achieved some level of worker solidarity, do they grab the dowel and beat her roundly about the head and shoulders? If so, she doesn't mention it.

The author says her "favorite" moment is when "the group becomes paralyzed. No one person wants to be the person to come off contact—so they don't take risks." Having induced this group paralysis, she then sets out to re-create the spirit of innovation and charismatic rule breaking, now as a function of the Team.

> *The most innovative groups question the "standing" start-ing point of the exercise. They notice that it's hard to make the switch from standing to the kneeling position that is re-quired to make the last move to the floor and keep in con-tact with the dowel. So they ask if they can start from a kneeling position. I generally approve this as I feel that the group is learning and questioning some unspoken rules.*[28]

So here is a group of people on their knees, finally. It was their own idea, erupting from the collective genius of the Team. Together, these mavericks develop the force of personality to "question some unspoken rules"—for example, that old canard that it's better to stand on your own two feet.

Given our democratic sensibilities, authority cannot present itself straightforwardly, *as* authority, coming down from a su-perior, but must be understood as an impersonal thing that emanates vaguely from all of us.[29] So authority becomes smarmy and passive-aggressive, trying to pass itself off as something co-operative and friendly; as volunteerism. It is always pretending to be in your best interest, in everyone's best interest, as ra-tionality itself.

The risk is of being deceived into thinking there is a com-mon good where there is not one. The fast-food worker seems to have the clearest view of this problem. He stakes his manly pride on maintaining his disengagement; on not devoting him-self to something that cannot profit him. Is such an approach to work really "pathological," as critics of the underclass insist, if there are no jobs for him that can engage his pride? Might the office worker balancing a wooden dowel on his finger not learn something important from the hamburger flipper?

Here we see the utility of the idea of corporate culture. The corporation has to become in the eyes of its employees something with transcendent meaning; something that can sustain the kind of moral demands normally associated with culture. Some notion of the common good has to be actively posited, a higher principle that can give people a sense of purpose in their work life. And indeed "organizational citizenship behavior," including a readiness to put "team objectives ahead of personal interests," is the new favorite personality measure of industrial psychologists.[30] This higher purpose typically remains on a meta-level, vaguely specified. Managers are instructed to generate it by talking about "higher purpose." But the absence of specific content to this higher purpose is its main feature. All the moral urgency surrounding it seems to boil down to an imperative to develop a disposition of teaminess.

When some worker doesn't recognize his own good in the collective good as defined by management and there is a conflict, that's when the therapeutic manager will take up the role of life coach, and turn his attention to the worker in a diagnostic mode. It is only natural, the worker is told, to feel *resistance*, especially to *change*. Everyone has *buttons* that will be pushed from time to time. But, the authors of *Teambuilding That Gets Results* ask, "[I]s it really the change that causes the stress? . . . Or is it our reactions to the new plan? . . . It may be true that the plan seems impossible, the unexpected turns make the job more difficult, and the radical ideas seem ridiculous, but stressing out or stewing only takes more energy that would be used more wisely toward adapting to the situation at hand."[31] Such stressing out or stewing indicates something amiss with the individual, his idiosyncratic hang-ups, not a reasonable reaction to an unreasonable situation. The reasonableness of the new situation is put beyond rational scrutiny, because change is a natural force, like metabolism: "98 percent of the atoms in your body are replaced every year; your skeleton is replaced every three months; your skin is replaced every four to five weeks," and so on.[32] The analogy suggests that when the job changes in a way that makes it more odious, it is not due to *decisions* that have been made by somebody, it is due to inexorable laws of nature. The very idea of responsibility is shown to be untenable.

There are activities that can be used to make the team confront its own attitudes toward change. Ask for five volunteers, and have them hold on to a long ribbon. Ask the person in the middle to start moving forward, then after forty-five seconds ask the group to stop. "Notice where each participant is. Discuss their reactions to the person moving forward. Some will have immediately followed, some will have stood their ground, others may have reluctantly been pulled along." Now it is time to process. Those who held back may have found the ribbon cutting into their hands; the ensuing discussion about how much it hurts to stay back is beneficial to all. On one occasion, a worker was reduced to tears, but with transformative effect. She explained that the exercise "put her resistance into perspective and she was ready to become fully engaged in taking the steps necessary to get her career back on track."[33]

The Crew versus the Team

Tocqueville foresaw a "soft despotism" in which Americans would increasingly seek their security in, and become dependent upon, the state. His analysis must be extended in our time: the softly despotic tendencies of a nanny state are found in the large commercial enterprise as well, and indeed a case could be made that it is now outsized corporations, more than government, that exercise this peculiarly enervating form of authority in our lives, through work.

Tocqueville also saw a remedy for this evil, however: the small commercial enterprise, in which Americans reason together to solve some practical problem among themselves. I believe this remedy remains valid, especially if the enterprise provides a good or service with objective standards, as these may serve as the basis for social relations within the enterprise that are nonmanipulative in character.

One way of getting at this possibility is to ask: How is being part of a *crew* different than being part of a "team" in the new mode of office work? The answer must lie, in part, in the ambiguous character of the thing produced in the latter. Say it is a marketing team at Apple. The success of the iPod, as a product, can't be specified in narrow engineering terms. Its success is due to the production of a new kind of behavior in consumers; we listen to music in a new way. The team's job is part of a large and complex enterprise, the object of which is to produce *culture*, and it is hard to get metrics of individual contributions to such an effort. Because of the scale and complexity of the undertaking, responsibility for success and failure are difficult to trace. There are no objective performance criteria to hold up before workers, but management still has to do *something*, so it directs its gaze to workers' mentalities, speaks of higher purpose, and brings in industrial psychologists to track various personality measures. For his part, the team member has no solid ground on which he can make a stand against this kind of moral training. He can't say, as the carpenter can to the foreman, "it's plumb and level—check it yourself." His only defense is a kind of self-division—he armors himself with the self-referential irony supplied to him by pop culture, pinning *Dilbert* cartoons to his cubicle wall and watching *The Office* every Thursday night.

There is pride of accomplishment in the performance of whole tasks that can be held in the mind all at once, and contemplated as whole once finished. In most work that transpires in large organizations, one's work is meaningless taken by itself. The individual feels that, alone, he is without any effect. His education prepares him for this; it is an education for working in a large organization, and he has difficulty imagining how he might earn a living otherwise. This predisposes him to be deferential to the authority exercised in the organization (however tinged with irony this deference may be), since the organization is that which gives meaning to his work.

Working in construction, one is similarly a part. Say you are an electrician. Your work of running circuits, then installing lights and switches and other devices, has no meaning outside the context of a whole building, with its walls built by the framers, its pipes and fixtures installed by a plumber, its foundation, roof, and all the rest. Taken separately, these trades are pointless; together you make accommodations for someone to live in. The difference is that on such a crew, you have grounds for knowing your own worth independently of others, and it is the same grounds on which others will make *their* judgments. Either you can bend conduit or you can't, and this is plain. So there is less reason to manage appearances. There is a real freedom of speech on a job site, which reverberates outward and sustains a wider liberality. You can tell dirty jokes. Where there is real work being done, the order of things isn't quite so fragile.

Not surprisingly, it is the office rather than the job site that has seen the advent of speech codes, diversity workshops, and other forms of higher regulation. Some might attribute this to the greater mixing of the sexes in the office, but I believe a more basic reason is that when there is no concrete task that rules the job—an autonomous good that is visible to all—then there is no secure basis for social relations. Maintaining consensus and preempting conflict become the focus of management, and as a result everyone feels they have to walk on eggshells. Where no appeal to a carpenter's level is possible, sensitivity training becomes necessary.[34]

The characteristic form of address on a job site is *command.* In the office, Jackall writes,

> managers' acute sense of organizational contingency makes them speak gingerly to one another since the person one criticizes or argues with today could be one's boss tomorrow. . . . Moreover, the crucial premium in the corporation on style

includes an expectation of a certain finesse in handling peo-
ple, a "sensitivity to others," as it is called. As one manager
says: "You can't just push people around anymore." Discreet
suggestions, hints, and coded messages take the place of com-
mand; this, of course, places a premium on subordinates'
abilities to read their bosses' vaguely articulated or com-
pletely unstated wishes.[35]

This sounds to me like being part of a clique of girls, where one can commit a serious misstep without knowing it; where one's place in the hierarchy is made difficult to know because of the forms and manners of sisterhood. Under such proprieties, even one's sense of being on probation may be difficult to bring to full awareness, taking instead the form of a dull and confusing anxiety.

The educational goal of self-esteem seems to habituate young people to work that lacks objective standards and revolves instead around group dynamics. When self-esteem is artificially generated, it becomes more easily manipulable, a product of social technique rather than a secure possession of one's own based on accomplishments. Psychologists find a positive correlation between repeated praise and "shorter task persistence, more eye-checking with the teacher, and inflected speech such that answers have the intonation of questions."[36] The more children are praised, the more they have a stake in maintaining the resulting image they have of themselves; children who are praised for being smart choose the easier alternative when given a new task.[37] They become risk-averse and dependent on others. The credential loving of college students is a natural response to such an education, and prepares them well for the absence of objective standards in the job markets they will enter; the validity of your self-assessment is known to you by the fact it has been dispensed by gatekeeping institutions. Prestigious fellowships, internships, and degrees become the standard of self-esteem. This is hardly an education for independence, intellectual adventurousness, or strong character.

"If you don't vent the drain pipe *like this*, sewage gases will seep up through the water in the toilet, and the house will stink of shit." In the trades, a master offers his apprentice good reasons for acting in one way rather than another, the better to realize ends the goodness of which is readily apparent. The master has no need for a psychology of persuasion that will make the apprentice compliant to whatever purposes the master might dream up; those purposes are given and determinate. He does the same work as the apprentice, only better. He is able to explain what he does to the apprentice, because there are rational principles that govern it. Or he may explain little, and the learning proceeds by example and imitation. For the apprentice there is a progressive revelation of the reasonableness of the master's actions. He may not know why things have to be done a certain way at first, and have to take it on faith, but the rationale becomes apparent as he gains experience. Teamwork doesn't have this progressive character. It depends on group dynamics, which are inherently unstable and subject to manipulation.

On a crew, skill becomes the basis for a circle of mutual regard among those who recognize one another as peers, even across disciplines. This may take the form of an actual circle at lunchtime, sitting on little coolers. An apprentice may aspire to be a journeyman so he can enter that circle, quite apart from considerations of pay. This is the basis on which his submission to the judgments of a master feel ennobling rather than debasing. There is a sort of friendship or solidarity that becomes possible at work when people are open about differences of rank, and there are clear standards.

7

Thinking as Doing

It is by having hands that man is the most intelligent of animals.

—ANAXAGORAS[1]

The nearest kind of association is not mere perceptual cognition, but, rather, a handling, using, and taking care of things which has its own kind of "knowledge."

—MARTIN HEIDEGGER[2]

Experienced firefighters know when to flee a burning building; it is not uncommon for them to leave moments before one collapses. When asked how they knew exactly when to leave, they fall back on ideas like "a sixth sense." The fact that the firefighters' intuitions strike us, and even themselves, as somehow otherworldly is a good indication that our understanding of how our minds grasp the world must be incomplete.

The current educational regime is based on a certain view about what kind of knowledge is important: "knowing that," as opposed to "knowing how." This corresponds roughly to universal knowledge versus the kind that comes from individual experience. If you know *that* something is the case, then this proposition can be stated from anywhere. In fact, such knowledge aspires to a view from nowhere. That is, it aspires to a view that gets at the true nature of things because it isn't conditioned by the circumstances of the viewer. It can be transmitted through speech or writing without loss of meaning, and expounded by a generic self that need not have any prerequisite experiences. Occupations based on universal, propositional knowledge are more prestigious, but they are also the kind that face competition from the whole world as book learning becomes more widely disseminated in the global economy. Practical know-how, on the other hand, is always tied to the experience of a particular person. It can't be downloaded, it can only be lived.

To parody the pretensions of theoretical knowledge, the ancient comedian Aristophanes coined a new word, *phrontisterion*. The literal translation is "think tank." In his play *Clouds* he has a distracted Socrates swing into view while suspended from a crane in a wicker basket, his gaze skyward. A supplicant has come, wishing to gain admission to Socrates' think tank. He calls out to Socrates from below. Socrates peers over the edge of his basket and responds.

Socrates: "Why dost thou call me, thou transient mortal?"

The would-be student: "First tell me: What the hell are you doing up there?"

Socrates: "I traverse the air and contemplate the sun."

The would-be student wonders why Socrates does these things from his contrived perch. "Why not do it from the ground, if at all?"

Socrates: "I could never have made correct discoveries about meteorological matters if I hadn't suspended my mind and infused the minute particles of my thought into the air, which it resembles. If I had been on the ground and merely gaped at the upper regions from below, I would never have made my discoveries. For the earth sucks the thought-juice down."[3]

We take a very partial view of knowledge when we regard it as the sort of thing that can be gotten while suspended aloft in a basket. This is to separate knowing from doing, treating students like disembodied brains in jars, the better to become philosophers in baskets—these ridiculous images are merely exaggerations of the conception of knowledge that enjoys the greatest prestige.

To regard universal knowledge as the whole of knowledge is to take no account of embodiment and purposiveness, those features of actual thinkers who are always in particular *situations*. The situated or worldly character of an embodied being has implications for the way we come to know the world, and the expert knowledge of the firefighter may be regarded as a heightened version of our everyday cognition. We do not usually encounter things in a disinterested way, for the simple reason that things that have no bearing on us do not engage our attention, of which we have a finite amount. ("Having a bearing on" must be taken generously; an attractive stranger who walks down the street as we sit at an outdoor café may engage our attention quite fully. As an object of desire, he or she bears on our world in the sense of opening up potential avenues of action, even if these are pursued only in the imagination.)

The things we know best are the ones we contend with in some realm of regular practice. Heidegger famously noted that the way we come to know a hammer is not by *staring* at it, but by grabbing hold of it and using it. For him, this was a deep point about our apprehension of the world in general. The pre-occupation with knowing things "as they are in themselves" he found to be wrongheaded, tied to a dichotomy between subject and object that isn't true to our experience. The way things actually "show up" for us is not as mere objects without context, but as equipment for action (like the hammer) or solicitations to action (like the beautiful stranger) within some worldly situation. One of the central questions of cognitive science, rooted in the prevailing epistemology, has been to figure out how the mind "represents" the world, since mind and world are conceived to be entirely distinct. For Heidegger, there is no problem of *re*-presenting the world, because the world *presents* itself originally as something we are already *in* and *of*. His insights into the situated character of our everyday cognition shed light on the kind of expert knowledge that is also inherently situated, like the firefighter's or the mechanic's.

If thinking is bound up with action, then the task of getting an adequate *grasp* on the world, intellectually, depends on our doing stuff in it. And in fact this is the case: to really know shoelaces, you have to tie shoes. Otherwise you might make the error my father did, attributing the properties of mathematical strings to shoelaces, and airily suppose that a double knot can be untied in one stroke, regardless of the particular material the shoelace is made of.[4] The economists Alan Blinder and Frank Levy have shown us the likely consequences, in an increasingly global labor market, of the fact that some jobs are inherently situated, and cannot be reduced to rule following. And I know from experience that the habits of mind of the mathematical physicist are ill suited to the realities of an old car. Let us consider more fully how it is that practical know-how is neither fully formalizable nor essentially rulelike.

Of Ohm's Law and Muddy Boots

One of the nuggets my dad offered me as I was trying to figure out why I was getting no spark at the spark plug, in my 1963 Volkswagen, was Ohm's law: $V=IR$, where V stands for voltage, I for current, and R for resistance. The equation states that these things stand in a definite relationship to one another. But in an old car, the idea of resistance as something simple and unitary, as the letter R, can get in the way of the kind of perception required to notice the actual sources of resistance, and the varied circumstances they are tied to. What mechanics say is that electrical connections need to be *tight*, *dry*, and *clean* of corrosion and dirt. They are constantly becoming loose from vibration, wet from the weather, corroded because that is the way of all flesh, and dirty because *the road is a dirty place*.

Ohm's law doesn't refer to any particular place, nor does it refer to the particular sources of corruption. Such as rain. During one of those rainy weeks when he keeps having to wipe the mud off his boots and peel a clammy shirt off his shoulders, an experienced mechanic facing an ignition problem in an older car is likely to reach for some WD-40 and spray it in the distributor, to displace moisture from the contact points. On the other hand, if his hair is full of sand that has been raining down in little micro-avalanches from the recesses of a truck up on the lift, he is likely to intuit that the driver has been off-roading in the local dunes, say, and reach instead for his compressed air to blow debris out of the distributor. I say "intuit" rather than "conclude" because he may not draw any explicit connections in his mind between muddy boots and remedy A, on the one hand, and sandy hair and remedy B, on the other. Rather, he is familiar with typical *situations*, and their typicality is something of which he has a *tacit* knowledge. This tacit knowledge seems to consist of recognizing patterns, and the causal patterns of the ignition problem are mirrored by patterns in his own bodily motions: periodically scratching the sand out of his scalp, or peeling a clammy shirt off his shoulders.

Ohm's law is something explicit and rulelike, and is true in the way that propositions are true. Its utter simplicity makes it beautiful; a mind in possession of this equation is charmed with a sense of its own competence. We feel we have access to something universal, and this affords a pleasure that is quasi-religious, perhaps. But this charm of competence can get in the way of noticing things; it can displace, or perhaps hamper the development of, a different kind of knowledge that may be difficult to bring to explicit awareness, but is superior as a practical matter. Its superiority lies in the fact that it begins with the typical rather than the universal, so it goes more rapidly and directly to particular causes, the kind that actually tend to cause ignition problems.

Appreciating the situated character of the kind of thinking

we do at work is important, because the degradation of work is often based on efforts to replace the intuitive judgments of practitioners with rule following, and codify knowledge into abstract systems of symbols that then stand in for situated knowledge. Daniel Bell, the author of *The Coming of Post-Industrial Society*, calls this codification an "intellectual technology." Its significance lies in the fact that it opens up the possibility of a "social technology," that is, a division of labor, that may be brought to bear on, for example, the organization of a hospital, an international trade system, or a work group whose members are engaged in specialized tasks for a common objective. The crux of the idea of an intellectual technology is "the substitution of algorithms (problem-solving rules) for intuitive judgments. These algorithms may be embodied in an automatic machine or a computer program or a set of instructions based on some statistical or mathematical formula."[5]

Bell seems to regard the mechanization and centralization of thinking as progress, or at any rate as inevitable; it is the only proper response to the growing complexity of society. His readiness to do away with the intuitive judgments of expert practitioners rests on the idea that such judgments are inadequate to complex systems that may involve

> *the interaction of too many variables for the mind to hold in correct order simultaneously. . . . [I]ntuitive judgments respond to immediate cause-and-effect relationships which are characteristic of simpler systems, whereas in complex systems the actual causes may be deeply hidden or remote in time or, more often, may lie in the very structure (i.e. pat-*

tern) of the system itself, which is not immediately recognizable. For this reason, one has to use algorithms, rather than intuitive judgments, in making decisions.[6]

Such a cognitive theory, if sound, would justify the alienation of judgment from skilled professionals when things get too complex. But, in fact, it is often the case that when things get really hairy, you want an experienced human being in control. The preference for algorithms over intuitive judgments, when faced with causes that "lie in the very structure (i.e. pattern)" of a system, is precisely the wrong conclusion to draw if one gives due regard to the tacit dimension of knowledge.

The Tacit Knowledge of the Firefighter and the Chess Master

The basic idea of tacit knowledge is that we know more than we can say, and certainly more than we can specify in a formulaic way. Intuitive judgments of complex systems, especially those made by experts, such as an experienced firefighter, are sometimes richer than can be captured by any set of algorithms.

The psychologist Gary Klein has studied the decision making of firefighters and other experts who perform complex tasks in the real world. "In many dynamic, uncertain, and fast-paced environments, there is no single right way to make decisions," Klein says. "Experts learn to perceive things that are invisible to novices, such as the characteristics of a typical situation."[7]

The experienced mind can get good at integrating an extraordinarily large number of variables and detecting a coherent pattern. It is the pattern that is attended to, not the individual variables. Our ability to make good judgments is holistic in character, and arises from repeated confrontations with real things: comprehensive entities that are grasped all at once, in a manner that may be incapable of explicit articulation.[8] This tacit dimension of knowledge puts limits on the reduction of jobs to rule following. It is not just the firefighter's *intervention* that is inherently in situ (as the economist Alan Blinder would point out). His knowledge, too, arises in particular places: places where there are fires.

Algorithms can be made to *simulate* the kind of tacit knowledge that experts possess, as when IBM's Deep Blue succeeded in playing chess at the highest level in 1997. Through brute computation of every possible move that adheres to the rules of chess (200 million board positions per second), the program was able to pick winning moves. To constrain the problem, the programmers made it their goal to beat one man in particular, Gary Kasparov, the reigning champion. Knowing his preferred opening moves and strategies made the problem tractable. But in beating Kasparov at his own game, Deep Blue was doing something very different than what a human chess player does. This is illustrated by an experiment in which an international chess master played speed chess with a limit of five seconds per move while also doing mental arithmetic. The arithmetic tied up his working memory and capacity for explicit analysis, yet he was still able to "more than hold his own" against "a slightly weaker, but master-level player."[9] Clearly, human chess players are doing something other than applying the rules of chess and comparing downstream board configurations along different decision trees, like a computer.

There is further evidence to suggest that what an expert human chess player *does* do is recognize patterns, like a firefighter. In a famous experiment, chess players of varying levels of competence viewed chess boards projected on a screen for a few seconds each.[10] They then had to reproduce the configuration of pieces they had seen. When the projected configurations were ones that actually occur in the game of chess, grandmasters were able to correctly reproduce the positions of twenty to twenty-five pieces, very good players about fifteen pieces, and beginners five or six. But when the pictures flashed before them showed random configurations of pieces, not corresponding to patterns they would have actually come across in playing chess, then there was no difference in the players' ability to reproduce the positions from memory; players of all levels were able to reproduce the positions of only five or six pieces.[11] The expert is expert not because he has a better memory in general, but because the patterns of chess are the patterns of his experience.

The success of Deep Blue would seem not to shed much light on how expert chess players do what they do. It might well be objected, "*of course* it doesn't; it's a computer!" This objection strikes me as just the right response, but sometimes common sense needs to be defended by an elaborate argument. We are constantly tempted to regard ourselves in the distorting mirror of technology, and in fact the "computational theory of mind" prevails in cognitive psychology (though it is becoming quite embattled).[12] An entire academic field has its origin in the idea that we *are* computers.[13] Further, the computer comes to represent an ideal, in light of which real thinking perversely begins to look deficient.[14] Thus, when the postindustrial visionary reasons from the fact that complex systems involve "the interaction of too many variables for the mind to hold in correct order simultaneously" to the conclusion that "one has to use algorithms, rather than intuitive judgments, in making decisions," he argues from the fact that the mind does not do what a computer does to an assertion about the incompetence of the mind. This seems to express an irrational prejudice against people. For, in fact, highly cultivated human minds can get to be pretty good at sussing out a burning building, playing chess, chasing down intermittent gremlins in a car's electrical system, and who knows what else.

The fact that a firefighter's knowledge is tacit rather than explicit, and therefore not capable of articulation, means that he is not able to give an account of himself to the larger society. He is not able to make a claim for the value of his mind in the terms that prevail, and may come to doubt it himself. But his own experience provides grounds for a radical critique of the view that theoretical knowledge is the only true knowledge.

Personal Knowledge versus Intellectual Technology

Tommy, my former shop mate, currently works at Pro Class Cycles, an independent shop on Richmond's south side that has been there since the mid-1980s. It is the place to go for used parts—the shop has about an acre of junk bikes. Bob Eubank, the proprietor, is known for good work at a fair price. The dealerships send him work that they know he can do more efficiently than their own employees, who are often recently out of the Motorcycle Mechanics Institute—building wheels, for example. Street bikes went to cast aluminum wheels in the late 1970s, but dirt bikes continue to have spoke wheels, and lacing one up can be a bewildering exercise in geometry. Bob's brother Lance, who also works there, is known to the dirt bike crowd as *the* guru for suspension tuning in central Virginia. He keeps his secrets even from his brother.

Bob is used to looking at something, say an internal engine part, and making a judgment about it based on experience—for example, looking at the first signs of glaze on a cylinder wall and judging whether it needs rehoning. Pressed to justify his decision, he might say, "I've seen them look like this and go another ten thousand miles without any loss of compression." The experience Bob relies on is very much his own; he is not following a set of instructions. When a mechanic makes this kind of judgment, he is relying on a tacit integration of sensual knowledge, by which he subconsciously refers what he sees to patterns built up in his mind through long experience. He does just what a firefighter and a chess master do.

Some modern motorcycles have begun to include onboard, computerized self-diagnostic functions, just as cars do. But they haven't eliminated the kind of judgment mechanics exercise. If we can understand *why* they haven't, this will help illuminate further the limitations inherent in the idea of an "intellectual technology," and the perversities that get laid upon work when those limitations aren't heeded.

Car manufacturers are supposed to standardize their diagnostics under a protocol called OBD-II (for onboard diagnostics), but as any mechanic will tell you, sometimes the system gives the wrong trouble code. Being off by one digit might give a diagnosis of "System fuel too lean on bank one" (P0171), that is, an air-fuel mixture that is too much air and not enough fuel on the first bank of cylinders, when in fact the problem is "System fuel too rich on bank two" (P0172). An experienced mechanic can tell too lean from too rich by looking at the spark plugs; they will look blanched white in the first case and sooty in the second. Representing states of the world in a merely formal way, as "information" of the sort that can be coded, allows them to be entered into a logical syllogism of the sort that computerized diagnostics can solve. But this is to treat states of the world in isolation from the context in which their *meaning* arises, so such representations are especially liable to nonsense. To rely entirely on computer diagnostics would put one in the situation of the schoolchild who learns to do square roots on a calculator without understanding the principle. If he commits a keying error while taking the square root of thirty-six and gets an answer of eighteen, it will not strike him that there is anything amiss. For the mechanic, the risk is that *someone else* committed a keying error.[15]

Computerized diagnostics don't so much replace the mechanic's judgment as add another layer to the work, one that requires a different sort of cognitive disposition. Tommy related the story of a late-model Kawasaki liter-class sport bike that came in. The customer reported that it was down on power, and there was an engine light flashing. Bob checked out the bike and could find nothing wrong, so he got ahold of the manufacturer's service manual for the bike, which gave instructions for retrieving a trouble code from the onboard diagnostic system. After this step you look up the code in a list to find out what the problem is.

The trouble code specified only that the issue was in the intake system, and directed him to a test procedure that would further narrow down the problem. In following the test procedure in the Kawasaki book, Bob got to a point where he said, "This is bullshit," and handed it off to Tommy. This is an important moment I would like to understand; we will return to it shortly.

Tommy worked through the procedure, which consisted of measuring impedances and voltages across various circuits and comparing them, as well as differences between pairs of them, to values listed in the book. He did this using a digital multimeter, which is the only way to get the precision you need. As anyone who has used such a meter knows, at the higher sensitivity settings used in much diagnostic work the reading tends to bounce around, and not in the way the old analog meters did, with the sweep of a pointer. With such a pointer the central value of, and variation in, the reading is represented spatially. With a digital multimeter what you sometimes get is a screen that won't settle down; it flashes different readings, often so quickly that you can't register them. Making matters worse, each of the ten digits is made up of little lines, just like in a digital watch (thus, an eight is a zero with an extra line across the middle, for example). As they flicker around, there is no inherent spatial mapping from what you see to the information represented. Sometimes it seems the screen's response is slower than the meter's time-wise integration of the underlying thermal noise that is generating the variation, so you get nonsense digits.[16] For example, you might get a backward nine. Or is that a *P*? What does that mean? Positive? Polarity?

The net effect on me is often the same as it was on Bob: "This is bullshit." The digital multimeter, together with the procedure in the book, present an image of precision and determinacy that is often false. What the procedure in fact demands of you is a real effort of interpretation, one that is nowhere acknowledged in the service manual.

But Tommy persisted. He had no choice; he was an employee. He got lots of ambiguous, unstable readings, so he repeated the test procedure several times. "I was looking for a difference in impedance in two different directions; I assumed there was some sort of diode in the sensor, but the book didn't actually tell me what had happened, just 'replace the expensive part' if the difference was less than a certain number." Such if-then logic aims to make the technician himself part of a mechanistic *replacement* for individual mind. At this moment Tommy's role was intended, by whoever conceived the service manual, to be that of a cog in the intellectual technology and corresponding social technology, rather than a thinking person.

The Service Manual as Social Technology

Service manuals were once written by people who worked on and lived with the machines they wrote about. At least one such writer achieved the status of sage and folk hero: John Muir, who wrote the manual I used when I first started working on VWs in 1980. I am sure that many thousands of other people remember his name as well, for his book is widely and rightly viewed as a classic.[17] He was an amateur in the best sense, and clearly had an intimate knowledge of Volkswagens. His treatment of mechanical problems wasn't divorced from the worldly situations in which they arise, and as a result the book is extraordinarily clear and useful. It has a human quality, as well.

The manuals written by professionals in previous decades were also very different than today's. They were written by engineers who were generally also mechanics and draftsmen, and it shows. The writer of the 1960 *Vincent Rider's Handbook* is anonymous, yet when he writes that one who has never ridden such a high-performance motorcycle before is "very prone to be deluded" in estimating his speed, you feel the presence of an actual human being, before whom you are willing to sit and learn. You look over this writer's shoulder as he describes the procedure for "grinding in" (that is, lapping) the valves. To be sure, you might wonder what exactly an Englishman means when he describes the sound of an engine as "wooly" (due to an overrich fuel mixture), but in looking at a drawing of the gearbox he might well have penned himself, the two of you enter into a common perception. It is a kind of philosophic friendship, the sort that is natural between teacher and student: a community of those who desire to know.

The intimacy of such a collaboration is part of the surplus that gets gathered as labor is fragmented. The writers of modern manuals are neither mechanics nor engineers but rather technical writers. This is a profession that is institutionalized on the assumption that it has its own principles that can be mastered without the writer being immersed in any particular problem; it is universal rather than situated. Technical writers know *that*, but they don't know *how*. They can be housed in an office building, and their work organized in the most efficient way possible. That is, in a way that generates the greatest volume of manual writing per staff member. In the case of Japanese motorcycles, you are further relying on some hapless Japanese student of English as a Second Language. This is my surmise, based on the nonsense these books invariably contain. You parse nonsensical or mutually contradictory sentences over and over again, trying to extract meaning from them by referring them, somehow, to the facts before you. If there are drawings involved, they will have been made by a person certified in a computer-aided drafting software suite, not by someone who knows what he is looking at, or what the situation and goal are likely to be for the person using the drawing. The mechanic has to peer through the mental fog introduced by these layers of fragmented, abstracted labor.[18]

To repeat, when Bob looks at a part and judges it to have ten thousand miles left on it, he is relying on a tacit integration of sensual knowledge, unconsciously referring what he sees to patterns built up in his mind through long experience. With computerized diagnostics, what is happening is rather an *explicit* integration of information, but this explicit integration is happening at the level of a knowledge system that is social in character. The *results* of this explicit integration are communicated to the mechanic by the service manual, written by people who have no personal knowledge of the motorcycle.

In John Searle's famous critique of artificial intelligence, he asks us to imagine a man locked in a room, with only a slit in the door connecting him to the outside word.[19] Through the door come pieces of paper with Chinese writing on them. The man does not know any Chinese. Unbeknownst to him, the writing takes the form of questions. He is equipped with a set of instructions, in English, for matching other Chinese symbols to the ones he is given. He passes these back through the slit, and they are taken to be answers to the questions. Searle's point is that to perform this task, the man needn't know any Chinese, and neither does a computer that does the same task as he. Some enthusiasts of artificial intelligence insist that *the system* knows Chinese—somehow there is thinking without a thinker. But a less mystical position would leave it at saying that it is the human programmer, who wrote up the instructions for matching Chinese answers to Chinese questions, who knows Chinese.

The mechanic relying on computerized diagnostics finds himself in a position similar to that of the man in the Chinese Room. The crucial stipulation in the thought experiment is that one could indeed have a set of rules that is fully adequate for matching answers to questions, without any reference to the meaning of the words being trafficked in. Whether this is in fact possible is a deep question in linguistics and philosophy of mind, and there is no noncontroversial answer to it. Yet the thoughtless way in which work is often conceived seems to presume the stipulation is correct. We view human beings as inferior versions of computers.

In Tommy's use of the test procedure on the Kawasaki, he *tried* to follow a set of rules, but in fact had to actively interpret a meter that wouldn't settle down, and a confusing manual. To get the bike back on the road, he had to render the gibberish coherent, and he could do this only by referring it to a model he had in his own mind of *how the thing works*.[20] The manual, the facts before him, and his prior knowledge of motorcycles had to be integrated into some coherent understanding. Otherwise he never would have been able to come to Bob and say, "I think I've got a diagnosis." What he conveyed with that announcement is that he had made a judgment. The "I think" part of Tommy's formulation can never be fully eliminated.

As an intended substitute for personal knowledge, the division of labor predicated on an "intellectual technology" presents a false pretense of rationality, one that the mechanic sometimes has to work *around* in order to do his job. It would be a mistake to suppose that this is a superficial problem that could be fixed by, for example, better training procedures for the technical writing staff. What they need is experience as mechanics. Otherwise what they produce is "a projection of thingness which, as it were, skips over the things," as Heidegger wrote in another context. Where the rubber meets the road, the mechanic is still responsible for the thing.

8

Work, Leisure, and Full Engagement

At the 1976 Olympics, the world was electrified by Nadia Comaneci's perfect 10.0 score in her gymnastics routine, which was unprecedented. In fact, the scoreboard was unable to register it—the possibility had not been anticipated, and read only to 9.99. The keeper of the scoreboard put up 1.00, and all understood. Reflecting on the event years later, Comaneci said, "During my routine and even after it, I did not think it was all that perfect. I thought it was pretty good, but athletes don't think about history when making history. They think about what they're doing, and that's how it gets done." Further, "I did not even look at the scoreboard when my routine was done in 1976. My teammates started pointing because there was this uproar."[1]

These remarks highlight an important feature of those practices that entail skilled and active engagement: one's attention is focused on standards intrinsic to the practice, rather than external goods that may be won through the practice, typically money or recognition. Can this distinction between internal and external goods inform our understanding of work?

It may be telling that it is leisure activities that come first to mind when we think about intrinsic satisfactions—athletics, for example, or hobbies that we enjoy. Such activities are ends in themselves, and we pursue them without anyone having to pay us to do so. Conversely, with work, getting paid is really the main point, and there would be something utopian in trying to understand work without reference to its external rewards. It may be that a partition of work and leisure, harsh necessity and sweet pursuits, is just a fact of life. But I want to consider what a more integral sort of life might look like, even if doing so requires venturing into the discreditable territory of "idealism."

It is common today to locate one's "true self" in one's leisure choices. Accordingly, good work is taken to be work that maximizes one's means for pursuing these other activities, where life becomes meaningful. The mortgage broker works hard all year, then he goes and climbs Mount Everest. The exaggerated psychic content of his summer vacation sustains him through the fall, winter, and spring. The Sherpas seem to understand their role in this drama as they discreetly facilitate his need for an unencumbered, solo confrontation with unyielding Reality. There is a disconnect between his work life and his leisure life; in the one he accumulates money and in the other he accumulates psychic nourishment. Each part depends on and enables the other, but does so in the manner of a transaction between sub-selves, rather than as the intelligibly linked parts of a coherent life.

On the other hand, there are vocations that seem to offer a tighter connection between life and livelihood. Can such coherence be traced to the nature of the work itself? A doctor deals with bodies, a fireman with fires, a teacher with children. Like Everest, these things are real enough, and the practices that serve them demand the kind of focused attention around which a life might take shape (as mountaineering does for the Sherpas). In these learned professions, the practitioner develops a highly discriminating appreciation of his objects, not unlike an aesthetic sense. His judgments of bodies, fires, children, or mountains become truer with experience, and therefore his ability to respond appropriately to them progresses.

The teacher who is really a teacher loves children, and wants to figure out how to make them smarter. Most people who get into working on cars do so because they love cars. Usually they want to figure out how to make them go faster. The work of a mechanic, then, may have the character of a vocation.

The Groove of the Speed Shop

The speed shop, such as Donsco, has been a fixture of American life for many decades. For those who work in such shops, like Chas, it seems hard to draw a line between job and leisure; it is a way of life. A speed shop usually consists of a storefront selling high-performance parts (domestic or import, never both) with a machine shop and a service bay in the back. There is a constant parade of blown-up or otherwise broken hoopties limping in, their drivers hoping to get things sorted by talking to the staff and other customers, buying parts and machining services, and (with utmost delicacy, if one wants not to be banished) borrowing tools. Many speed shops take on the character of a clubhouse, and will campaign a race car or two in whatever motor sport they are into.

Often someone working at a speed shop spent his younger days lingering around the counter, then, as he penetrated the social hierarchy, in the back, allowed now to pull his car around and perhaps use a floor jack to install some shock absorbers purchased at the counter. Such an exposure to injury liability would give a lawyer fits; implicit in the invitation to the back is a judgment of the young man's character and a large measure of trust. He will get some light supervision that is likely to be disguised as a stream of sexual insults, delivered from ten feet away by someone he cannot see (only his shoes) as he lies under his car. Such insults are another index of trust. If he is able to return these outrageous comments with wit, the conversation will cascade toward real depravity; the trust is pushed further and made reciprocal. If the young man shows promise, that is, if he is judged to have some potential to plumb new depths of moral turpitude, he may get hired: here is someone around whom everyone can relax.

The fringe benefit of a discount on parts, and the use of a lift after hours for his own car, is a big part of the compensation. Having the next crop of kids coming in and seeking his advice is no doubt another part; he rises in stature. Showing up at, say, the local dirt track oval on a Saturday night, with his shop's posse in matching T-shirts, is another pleasure. Or maybe the whole crew caravans down to Baja for one of the big desert races, with a train of hangers-on. Guys will glom on to the scene by dignifying their rides as "chase vehicles" or "pre-runners," the idea being to run the course ahead of time to check it out. It's a day and night festival reeking of high-test race gas and warm beer, punctuated by the breaking of metal.

The social hierarchy is tied to a speed ethic that can be a little challenging for a younger man to decode. He may need to be schooled. When I was eighteen, about a year after being inducted into the Volkswagen speed scene by Chas, I was parked in front of another shop, the Buggy House in Hayward, messing with the carburetor that protruded through a hole I'd cut in the deck lid of my car—a crudely ostentatious approach. A guy in a bone stock-looking Bug pulls up, parks, and goes into the shop. He was older. After a few minutes he comes out and gets back in his car, without saying a word. I was hoping he'd seen my fancy Italian carb. He starts the car, which emanates a quiet, mild-mannered sound. Then he puts it in first gear and proceeds to light up the tires.

Now he jams it into second. The car is still not moving forward, but the cloud of white smoke billowing out from the fenders is getting denser, and the rear end is starting to drift to one side. He speed shifts into third and finally the car starts to move forward, slowly and in a direction that is still vague, as I stand there agog. The tires melt and get sticky, the rear end squats, the car launches and, after traveling about thirty yards, he hits fourth and gets a good chirp, a sort of parting comment. The smoke hung in the dead summer air, a compact cloud that drifted toward me in eerie silence. As the stench of burning rubber reached my nostrils, I began to understand what people mean when they call a car a "sleeper." That would be the opposite of "all show and no go." It's not just how fast you go, it's how you go fast. I felt a bit like a puppy who'd gotten a rolled-up newspaper across the nose.

Community

Can the speed shop teach us anything about the tension between work and leisure, and how it might be eased in the direction of a coherent life? It is a community of consumption that overlaps with a community of work. The overlap takes place within the life of each participant, and the shop is the site where the overlap becomes social: no one working there isn't also an enthusiast, and no customer isn't deeply involved with the nuts and bolts of his own car. They know the particulars of each other's engines. A machinist working at a speed shop is likely to see the same crankshaft several times over the years. He will recognize his own writing on the counterweights, in grease pen or Sharpie, noting the bearing tolerances with each rebuild as its journals get ground and polished. He may have witnessed the same motor blow up over the weekend, and decide to experiment with a different length of connecting rod. Everyone is progressing in knowledge, through a shared dialectic. The dialectic is between people, but also between iterations—you break things, and learn something new by taking them apart and talking it through. Here work and leisure both take their bearings from something basically human: rational activity, in association with others. This activity is directed toward something that appears as good within the horizon of a certain way of life: *speed.* To place oneself in the service of this master is to enter into a community and, as I learned outside the Buggy House, to open oneself to being schooled by one's elders. This is solidarity.

I believe the question of whether work is "alienated" or not may be understood in terms of the kind of perception it affords. Marx held that it is through work that we realize our "species character," and this consists in our being both rational and social beings. For him it follows that we get alienated from ourselves when the product of our work is appropriated, since that product is a concrete manifestation of one's own most human possibilities. The worker's product is "torn away" from him, and Marx suggests that it becomes an alien thing, hateful to him, because it is *used* by another. But why should this be? I find Marx unconvincing on this point. If I am a furniture builder, for example, what am I going to do with a hundred chairs? After all, I want to *see them in use*; this completes my activity of making them, and gives it social reality. It makes me feel I have contributed to the common good. But as the philosopher Talbot Brewer suggests, this raises the question of how direct the perception of use must be, if it is to play this role.

It is one thing for the Chinese factory worker to know that somewhere in the U.S. hinterlands, the vernacular rural American quilt that she has stitched together is being used, and that it has some culturally specific significance to the

person using it, which she can barely comprehend. It is an-
other thing for a carpenter to walk around a town and see
the new entryway he designed and built for that *store, to*
learn from a direct experience and from chatting with oth-
ers of its functional and aesthetic achievements and short-
comings, and to modify future work in accordance with this
running feedback that is picked up in the course of daily ac-
tivities. There are, of course, a world of possibilities between
these two extremes. One might read Marx as having ges-
tured, at least, towards the plausible thought that the nearer
one is to the carpenter's end of this continuum, the less alien-
ated one is from one's own work.[2]

When the maker's (or fixer's) activity is immediately situated
within a community of use, it can be enlivened by this kind of
direct perception. Then the social character of his work isn't
separate from its internal or "engineering" standards; the work
is improved *through* relationships with others. It may even be
the case that what those standards *are*, what perfection consists
of, is something that comes to light only through these iterated
exchanges with others who use the product, as well as other
craftsmen in the same trade. Through work that has this social character, some shared conception of the good is lit up,
and becomes concrete.

The geographical and cultural estrangement of the Chinese
quilt maker precludes this kind of experience. There is another
form estrangement may take: use may be utterly separate from
production under conditions of radical inequality, even within
the same city. This is especially so in the case of luxury goods,

and it is plausible that someone in Beijing stitching together designer handbags for the plutocrats of that same city would find them hateful.

Consider how a similar set of facts may carry a different meaning when the inequality is overlaid with some sense of a *res publica*, or common wealth. Consider a panel beater who shapes sheet metal for Rolls-Royce, circa 1970. He could never afford to own one of the cars he makes, but he participates in the greatness of Rolls-Royce, and feels himself enlarged by it. The company has a national character: Britain's best. Likewise consider the Mercedes worker, who feels the pride of "German engineering" as his own. The product is still "torn away" by a different class, as Marx says, yet there is a political community, distinct from the market, where we locate a common good. Ideas of national greatness, often tied to material culture, once sustained common identities that mitigated class antagonism to some degree—being an Englishman. The Marxist would fully agree, but put a negative cast on such identity as an obstacle to revolution. For him nationalism is an ideology that keeps the working classes down by preventing the development of class consciousness. But the pride of the Rolls-Royce panel beater gives his work human dignity, and the Marxist is presumptuous to call it "false consciousness."

Ironically, it is now the managerial elite of international capital that is likely to complain of the false consciousness of those workers on whom the idea of the nation retains some grip (for example, those who oppose easy immigration). It is now the capitalist who says, "Workers of the world, unite!," the better to dissolve those "inefficiencies" in the labor market (that is, high wages) that arise from political boundaries. The slogan once expressed a hope to organize a body of workers who were dispersed and hence exploitable, whereas now it captures the desire for a mass of "human resources," exploitable because undifferentiated. This latter intention is accompanied by all the easy moral prestige of multiculturalism, so it finds its champions on the erstwhile Left. Those at the top of the food chain get a new identity in which to take pride, that of the sushi-eating, Brazilian-girlfriend-having cosmopolitan. But what does the autoworker get as industries lose their national character? It is harder to take pride in one's work as "a Rolls-Royce man," for example, if the car is assembled from parts made who knows where.

One remedy is to find work in the cracks; work the market rationale of which is fully contained within a human scale of face-to-face interactions. This is what the speed shop offers; it is a community of making and fixing that is embedded within a community of use. Such enterprises are not "scalable" in the way that whets the appetite of remote investors, much as they might like to explode the happy scene and "take it global."

These reflections on the role of community in meaningful work needn't be confined to the manual trades. Consider once again our hypothetical Everest-climbing mortgage broker. First, imagine an older version of the banker. In the nineteenth century, there was a prohibition in the United States on banks opening branches in communities other than the ones in which they originally operated. People had to trust the bank if they were to deposit their money in it, and bankers had to assess the character of borrowers before writing loans; it was generally believed that "the bankers' interests and the interests of the larger community are one and the same," as a historical sociologist of banking writes.[3] We might imagine a banker sits down with a young couple and begins to form a judgment of their creditworthiness, that is, their character. This character is knowable because there is a community. Maybe the banker asks around at the grocery and the hardware store, and notes subtle cues in the tone of voice or body language of their proprietors as he mentions the names of the applicants, and inquires after their record of credit. Satisfied, he vouchsafes their creditworthiness to his colleague bankers, who live in the same community, and a mortgage is secured. A thirty-year relationship is established between the bank and the couple. The banker feels he has done a good turn, helping virtue to its reward by the diligent application of his own powers of discerning observation, and his knowledge of the ways of men. He exercises prudence; his work calls on some of his best capacities. As Thomas Lamont, the head of J. P. Morgan & Co., put it to his colleagues in 1923, customers' faith in a bank isn't simply based on a presumption of honesty. Rather, "the community as a whole demands of the banker that he shall be an honest observer of conditions about him, that he shall make constant and careful study of those conditions, financial, economic, social and political, and that he shall have a wide vision over them all."[4]

Now consider the reality of the mortgage broker circa 2005, whose work takes on a very different character under absentee capitalism. Knowing the mortgage he secures will be sold by the originating bank (a branch of a nationwide bank) to some other entity, he needn't concern himself with the creditworthiness of the applicant. The bank has no interest in the ongoing viability of the loan; its interest is limited to the fees it gets from originating the loan. The mortgages will be bundled on Wall Street, then these bundles will themselves be transformed through securitization into quantized particles of something more general, "housing debt," and sold to the Chinese government and other investors. The original encounter between mortgage broker and borrower as they sit across from one another is fraught with moral content—questions of trust—and both of the original parties no doubt experience it this way, in 2005 as ever. The mortgage broker gets a feeling in his gut. But this information is discarded through a process of depersonalization. The discarding is purposeful.[5] Indeed, the originating banks get frequent phone calls from Wall Street investment houses, urging them to invent new kinds of loans in which the borrower doesn't even need to *claim* income or assets, much less prove their existence.[6] This makes a certain kind of psychic demand on the mortgage broker who actually writes the loans: he must silence the voice of prudence, and suspend the action of his own *judgment* and *perception*.

Why would a system demand the stupidification of the mortgage professional? Again, imagine it is 2005. Unprecedented concentrations of capital have arisen, and these pools of money are competing with one another to find a home, and get a return. As a result there is an insatiable worldwide appetite for mortgage-backed securities among investors. Further, the fees to be made from all the transactions between originator and investor are fueling a Wall Street boom. Therefore *more loans must be written.* So our mortgage broker writes loans that he knows to be bad, and makes a lot of money. Stripped of the kind of judgments that are at the very heart of the idea of "credit," shot through with bad faith, his work is now predicated on irresponsibility, rooted in the absence of community. Whatever lingering fiduciary consciousness he may have has become a liability, given the general rush to irresponsibility by his competitors. The work cannot sustain him as a human being. Rather, it damages the best part of him, and it becomes imperative to partition work off from the rest of life. So during his vacation he goes and climbs Mount Everest, and feels renewed. The next summer, he becomes an ecotourist in the Amazon rain forest. It is in this gated ghetto of his second life that he inhabits once again an intelligible moral order where feeling and action are linked, if only for a couple of weeks.

Wholehearted Activity

Aristotle's understanding of happiness can shed light on those activities that truly engage us; maybe it can teach us something about work and leisure as well. His account is grounded in a more comprehensive understanding of creatures: to understand any particular sort of being, the best way to proceed is by *looking* at it, and taking note of its characteristic activity. That activity represents the "end" of the creature, its purpose. In Greek, its *telos.* In English, this teleological understanding of happiness gets condensed in the proverbial saying "Happy as a pig in shit." Rolling around in shit is what pigs do, and they dig it. Frolicking is what dolphins do. It is worth noting in passing how Aristotle's biology reverses the contemporary Darwinian view. For the neo-Darwinian, the frolicking of the dolphin is assumed to have some survival value, either for the preservation of the individual or for the passing on of its genes. I suspect that if you were to ask a dolphin about this, he would say it is backward: he lives in order to frolic, he doesn't frolic in order to live. This is the Aristotelian view, precisely. Such activities are experienced as intrinsically good. They contain their end within themselves; they *enact* that end, in "real time," as we now say.

The mucking of the pig and the frolicking of the dolphin would seem to be leisure activities. Yet many animals do things that look a lot like work, changing nature's forms to make them useful. The bird builds its nest, the spider its web. Some even use rudimentary tools—for example, an otter may use a rock to smash open abalone, or a chimpanzee a stick to retrieve termites. Thomas Hobbes suggested the human difference lies in the fact that animals begin with a desired effect and discover a sufficing instrument, whereas we are capable of viewing everything as a potential instrument and imagining all the effects to which it could potentially give rise, corresponding to wildly different ends. For humans, tools point to the necessity of moral inquiry. Because nature makes only ambiguous prescriptions for us, we are compelled to ask, what is good? If you give a young boy a hammer for the first time and watch his face, you will see an awareness of this burden dawning on him (as he turns to the cat, for example).

So there is an aspect of inquiry that hovers about our practical activities, which may or may not be brought to full awareness and issue in careful reflection. Following Aristotle, Brewer connects this aspect of inquiry to our experience of pleasure, the kind we get when we become absorbed in what we are doing (like Comaneci on the balance beam). He writes that there is an "appreciative discernment of value that accompanies and carries forward intrinsically valuable activities," and that it is this evaluative attention that renders the activity pleasurable. "[T]o take pleasure in an activity is to engage in that activity while being absorbed in it, where this absorption consists in single-minded and lively attention to whatever it is that seems to make the activity good or worth pursuing. . . . If one were struck only by the instrumental value of the activity . . . one's evaluative attention would be directed not at the activity but at its expected results—that is, at something other than what one is doing. This sort of attention . . . absents us from our activity and renders it burdensome."[7]

There is a classic psychology experiment that seems to confirm Brewer's point. Children who enjoy drawing were given marker pens and allowed to go at it. Some were rewarded for drawing (they were given a certificate with a gold seal and a ribbon, and told ahead of time about this arrangement), whereas for others the issue of rewards was never raised. Weeks later, those who had been rewarded took less interest in drawing, and their drawings were judged to be lower in quality, whereas those who had not been rewarded continued to enjoy the activity and produced higher-quality drawings. The hypothesis is that the child begins to attribute his interest, which previously needed no justification, to the external reward, and this has the effect of reducing his intrinsic interest in it.[8] That is, an external reward can affect one's interpretation of one's own motivation, an interpretation that comes to be self-fulfilling. A similar effect may account for the familiar fact that when someone turns his hobby into a business, he often loses pleasure in it. Likewise, the intellectual who pursues an academic career gets professionalized, and this may lead him to stop thinking.

This line of reasoning suggests that the kind of appreciative attention where one remains focused on what one is doing can arise only in leisure activities. Such a conclusion would put pleasurable absorption beyond the ken of any activity that is undertaken for the sake of making money, because although money is undoubtedly good, it is not intrinsically so. It represents a generic potency; the goodness of money floats free of any *particular* evaluations that could engage our attention and energize our activity. Keeping in mind some specific good to be acquired (such as an opportunity to climb Mount Everest) doesn't solve this problem; such imaginings cannot imbue the work itself with mindfulness, and are likely to have the opposite effect of making us stand apart from the job. Sadly, this may be just what is wanted.

But all this is perhaps too categorical. For in fact, there are people who enjoy their work. You can earn money at something without the money, or what it buys, being the focus of your day. To be capable of sustaining our interest, a job has to have room for progress in excellence. In the best cases, I believe the excellence in question ramifies outward. What I mean is that it points to, or serves, some more comprehensive understanding of the good life.

I like to fix motorcycles more than I like to wire houses (even though I could make about twice as much money wiring houses).[9] Both practices have internal goods that engage my attention, but fixing bikes is more meaningful because not only the fixing but also the *riding* of motorcycles answers to certain intuitions I have about human excellence. People who ride motorcycles have gotten something *right*, and I want to put myself in the service of it, this thing that we do, this kingly sport that is like war made beautiful.

My job of making motorcycles run right is subservient to the higher good that is achieved when one of my customers leans hard through a corner on the Blue Ridge Parkway, to the point of deliberately dragging his well-armored knee on the inside. This moment of faith, daring, and skill casts a sanctifying light over my work. I try to get his steering head bearings as light and silky as they can be without free play, and his swing arm bushings good and tight, because I want him to feel his tires truly. Only then can he make the road fully his own. If I am riding twenty yards behind him, I want to *hear* the confidence he has in the chassis I have tuned, expressed by the way he rolls on the throttle, brashly, through the exit of a turn. He is likely to pull away from me; I may find him waiting for me at Cumberland Gap with a verdict that lighter fork oil is called for, to get less damping in the front end.

I try to be a good motorcycle mechanic. This effort connects me to others, in particular to those who exemplify good motorcycling, because it is they who can best judge how well I have realized the functional goods I am aiming at.[10] I wouldn't even know what those goods *are* if I didn't spend time with people who ride at a much higher level than I, and are therefore more discerning of what is good in a motorcycle.[11] So my work situates me in a particular community. The narrow mechanical things I concern myself with are inscribed within a larger circle of meaning; they are in the service of an activity that *we* recognize as part of a life well lived. This common recognition, which needn't be spoken, is the basis for a friendship that orients by concrete images of excellence.

My point, finally, isn't to recommend motorcycling in particular, nor to idealize the life of a mechanic. It is rather to suggest that if we follow the traces of our own actions to their source, they intimate some understanding of the good life. This understanding may be hard to articulate; bringing it more fully into view is the task of moral inquiry. Such inquiry may be helped along by practical activities in company with others, a sort of conversation in deed. In this conversation lies the potential of work to bring some measure of coherence to our lives.

Concluding Remarks on
Solidarity and Self-Reliance

This book grows out of an attempt to get a critical handle on my own work history; to understand the human possibilities latent in what I was doing when the work seemed good, and when it was bad to identify the features of the work that systematically preempted or damaged those same possibilities. In sorting these things out, we have had occasion to think about the nature of rationality, the conditions for individual agency, the moral aspect of perception, and the elusive ideal of community.

Do the arguments I have made about meaningful work necessarily point to the trades? If we accept the testimony of the early-twentieth-century banker Thomas Lamont, related in chapter 8, his work was founded on direct perceptions, a "wide vision" over the community, issuing in judgments of better and worse character—the sort of evaluative attention that can join us to our work as full-blooded human beings. But as the subsequent history of banking illustrates, any job that can be scaled up, depersonalized, and made to answer to forces remote from the scene of work is vulnerable to degradation, even to the point of requiring that the person who does the job actively suppress his better judgment.

The special appeal of the trades lies in the fact that they resist this tendency toward remote control, because they are inherently situated in a particular context. In the best cases, the building and fixing that they do are embedded in a community of using. Face-to-face interactions are still the norm, you are responsible for your own work, and clear standards provide the basis for the solidarity of the crew, as opposed to the manipulative social relations of the office "team." There are surely other kinds of work that I am unacquainted with where these goods can be realized; it remains for others to explore them.

Aristotle begins his *Metaphysics* with the observation that "all human beings by nature desire to know." I have argued that real knowledge arises through confrontations with real things. Work, then, offers a broadly available premonition of philosophy. Its value, however, does not lie solely in pointing to some more rarefied experience. Rather, in the best cases, work may itself approach the good sought in philosophy, understood as a way of life: a community of those who desire to know.

Solidarity and the Aristocratic Ethos

When I was sixteen, I traveled to India by myself. Stepping off the plane into the swelter of Bombay, I smelled something foreign and foul: burning garbage, I learned later. Rather than stand in a queue at the bus stop, the Indians mobbed the place where they expected the bus to be. They pressed against me uncomfortably, and they, too, stank—I felt utterly apart from people who were literally touching me. Their eyes looked dull, as though they didn't open into the same kind of chamber of consciousness as mine.

The next day, the rickshaw I was riding in stopped at a red light next to a construction site. There I saw some men wearing sandals and smoking tiny little cigarettes. They had spools of wire set up in a row, their hollow centers threaded onto a broomstick suspended between two crates. With a shock of recognition, I realized they were getting ready to pull wires through conduit. The dark thoughts of estrangement that absorbed me fled; I wanted to leap out of the rickshaw and say, "I do this, too!" Suddenly I felt connected to this small group of electricians. I wondered what they would use for lubricant (in America we use Ideal Yellow 77). I wondered if they used the same technique for constructing the "head" of the mass of wires to be pulled through (it needs to be as streamlined as possible). I wondered if they made the same, inevitable sexual jokes. I saw that they had the burliest guy, a Sikh to judge from his headgear, stationed at the other end of the conduit to do the actual pulling, just like in America. The oppressive sense that I was a foreigner among foreigners evaporated as I projected myself imaginatively into their day, into this very moment. They were currently encountering the world in a way that was familiar to me, orienting to it through a set of concerns I knew well, and the consciousness behind their eyes I took to be the same as my own.

"Obligation to others" is the claim made on us by various

systems of universal ethics. It has a dreary quality to it, like a summons for jury duty. The Kantians claim to find the source of this obligation in a rigorous argument, but I am not able to follow it. By contrast, *solidarity* with others is a positive attraction, akin to love. It is not an abstract imperative, but an actual experience we have from time to time. Its scope is necessarily smaller, its grip on our affections tighter, than that of any vaporous universal.

There is, in fact, something called the International Brotherhood of Electrical Workers. It is not very international; the union has members in the United States and Canada. But the name captures pretty well my experience of brotherhood in the rickshaw. That experience suggests an alternative to various attempts that have been made, along universalist lines, to mitigate the self-enclosure of the modern individual.

Today's liberal humanitarian posits human rights, based in a common humanity, as the ground of an obligation to distant others. This is a noble ideal, but perhaps too much so to engage our affections. When the humanity of others who were previously invisible becomes apparent to us for the first time, I think it is because we have noticed something particular in them. This may be some everyday experience we share with them, such as that of pulling wire, or it may be something unfamiliar that arrests our attention for being impressive—something *excellent*.

A regard for human excellence is the aristocratic ethos. To speak of aristocracy is perhaps a bit eccentric in our time, but consider the paradoxical truth that *equality* is an aristocratic ideal. It is the ideal of friendship—of those who stand apart from the collective and recognize one another as peers. As professionals, or fellow journeymen, perhaps. By contrast, the bourgeois principle is not equality but equivalence—a positing of interchangeability that elides human differences of rank.

This train of thought can help us to a clearer conscience about our aristocratic intuitions: such intuitions may humanize and deepen, rather than threaten, our democratic commitments. People of aristocratic sympathies are alive to rank and difference, and take pleasure in beholding them. I think most of us have this response when we see talent, but we have become inarticulate about it. It seems illegitimate to give rank its due in a society where "all children are above average," as Garrison Keillor says of Lake Woebegon. Yet it is precisely our attraction to excellence—our being on the lookout for the choicer manifestations—that may lead us to attend to human practices searchingly, without prejudice, and find superiority in unfamiliar places. For example, in the intellectual accomplishments of people who do work that is dirty, such as the mechanic. With such discoveries we extend our moral imagination to people who are conventionally beneath serious regard, and find them admirable. Not because we heed a moral injunction such as the universalist egalitarian urges upon us, but because we actually see something admirable, and are impressed by it.

The lover of excellence is prone to being drawn out of himself, erotically almost, in a way that the universalist egalitarian is not. The latter's empathy, projected from afar and without discrimination, is more principled than attentive. It is similar to bad art and mathematical shoelaces, in this regard; it is content to posit rather than to see the humanity of its beneficiaries. But the one who is on the receiving end of such empathy wants something more than to be recognized generically. He wants to be seen as an individual, and recognized as worthy on the same grounds on which he has *striven* to be worthy, indeed superior, by cultivating some particular excellence or skill.

The Importance of Failure

The practitioner of a stochastic art, such as motorcycle repair, experiences failure on a daily basis. Just today, for example, before sitting down to write, I was faced with a mangled screw frozen in a cylinder head. I had to cut the head of the screw off with a pneumatic chisel (easy enough), center punch the remaining stud (ditto), then drill it out with a cobalt drill bit. This last step is always dicey, and in fact the drill bit broke off inside the hole I was drilling. As far as I know there is no drill bit harder than cobalt that I can use to drill out the broken-off drill bit. (Apologies to Bob Gorman, the owner of this particular cylinder head—I'll make it right somehow.) Everything is going along swimmingly, then I find myself with no way forward. Such failures get internalized, and give rise to both pessimism and self-reproach. *Not only do things tend to go to hell, but your own actions contribute inevitably to that process.*

Those who belong to a certain order of society—people who make big decisions that affect all of us—don't seem to have much sense of their own fallibility. Being unacquainted with failure, the kind that can't be interpreted away, may have something to do with the lack of caution that business and political leaders often display in the actions they undertake on behalf of other people. In his book *Real Education*, Charles Murray relates a maxim attributed to Lyndon Johnson's press secretary: "No one should be allowed to work in the West Wing of the White House who has not suffered a major disappointment in life." Murray adds that "the responsibility of working there was too great . . . to be entrusted to people who weren't painfully aware of how badly things can go wrong."[1]

Yet, as Murray argues, the experience of failure seems to have been edited out of the educational process, at least for gifted students. Those who struggle academically experience failure all the time, and probably write off attempts to sugarcoat it with "self-esteem" as another example of how deranged adults can be. But the praising of gifted students for being smart, by parents and teachers, has a far more pernicious effect, especially when such praise is combined with the grade inflation and soft curriculum that are notorious at elite schools. A student can avoid hard sciences and foreign languages and get a degree without ever having the unambiguous experience of *being wrong*.

Such an education dovetails with the pedagogical effects of the material culture inhabited by the well-to-do, which insulates them from failed confrontations with hard reality. Such failures often force you to ask a favor of someone else, like when your car breaks down somewhere and you have no cell phone, and you have to flag down a motorist or knock on a door. Such an experience of dependence makes you humble, and grateful.

There may be something to be said, then, for having gifted students learn a trade, if only in the summers, so that their egos will be repeatedly crushed before they go on to run the country. But now I seem to be caught in a contradiction. Haven't I recommended the trades based on the *pride* they instill? Haven't I argued for self-reliance, and against dependence?

Individual Agency in a Shared World

I have tried to make a case for self-reliance of a certain kind—being master of your own stuff. This requires a basic intelligibility to our possessions: in their provenance, in their principles of operation, in their logic of repair and maintenance, in short, in all those ways that a material object can make itself fully manifest to us, so we can be responsible for it.

But viewed from a wider angle, self-reliance is a sad doctrine, arguably a consolation for the collapse of institutions of mutual care.[2] Pensions routinely fail, as do marriages. One bravely writes a living will so as not to be a burden on others. Family bonds give way to social security, which in turn gives way to the individual retirement account. To fill the void that comes with isolation, and give it a positive cast, we posit the ideal of the sovereign self, unencumbered by attachments to others and radically free. This is the consumer self that puts its stamp on the world by buying things, thereby giving an active expression to its preferences. These ideals of freedom and choice exert a powerful positive attraction, so there is perhaps a feedback loop whereby our isolation and our sovereign self-image mutually escalate. The same ethic of freedom is evident in the political or business executive who, with little sense of his own fallibility and how badly things can go wrong, acts on behalf of others without any pressing sense of concern. Given this broader problem of solipsism, why do I feel it necessary to make a case for self-reliance?

The kind of self-reliance I have in mind is essentially different from the cult of the sovereign self, and it requires some further reflection on the idea of agency. The concept of agency is often understood with reference to activity that is self-directed, rather than dictated by another. This distinction has an immediate appeal, but is liable to lead us astray in a characteristically modern way. "Self-directed" activity is usually taken to mean activity directed by the will of a self that simply chooses according to its whim. So the usual opposition is between ends dictated by another and ends dictated by the self. Labor predicated on the first is alienated; that predicated on the second is said to entail self-actualization or fulfillment.

The idea of agency I have tried to illustrate in this book is different. It is activity directed toward some end that is affirmed as good by the actor, but this affirmation is not something arbitrary and private. Rather, it flows from an apprehension of real features of the world. This may be something easy to grasp, as when a master plumber shows his apprentice that he has to vent a drain pipe a certain way so that sewage gases don't seep up through a toilet and make a house stink. Or it may be something requiring discernment, as when a better motorcyclist than I explains, from a rider's point of view, why it would be good to decrease the damping in the front end of his motorcycle. In activities that are directed toward some end (a well-vented drain pipe, a balanced chassis), the goodness of the end in question isn't simply posited. There is a progressive *revelation* of *why* one ought to aim at just this, as well as how one can achieve it. As you learn your trade this particular end takes its place in a larger picture that is emerging, a picture of what it means to be a good plumber or a good mechanic. Usually there is a real flesh-and-blood person who embodies this ideal, whom you emulate (as I did Chas, and later Fred). The progressive character of the revelation energizes your efforts to become competent—something about the world is coming into clearer view, and it is exciting. The sense that your judgments are becoming truer is part of the experience of being fully engaged in what you are doing; it is a feeling of joining a world that is independent of yourself, with the help of another who is further along.

A carpenter faces the accusation of his level, an electrician must answer the question of whether the lights are in fact on, a speed shop engine builder sees his results in a quarter-mile time slip. Such standards have a universal validity that is apparent to all, yet the discriminations made by practitioners of an art respond also to aesthetic subtleties that may not be visible to the bystander. Only a fellow journeyman is entitled to say "nicely done." A judgment on the finer points can arise only within, and receives its force and justification from, a shared orientation toward the more basic functional ends that are captured by the objective standards of the practice. It is in doing the job nicely that the tradesman puts his own stamp on it. His individuality is not only compatible with, it is realized *through* his efforts to reach a goal that is common.

His individuality is thus expressed in an activity that, in answering to a shared world, connects him to others: the customers he serves and other practitioners of his art, who are competent to recognize the peculiar excellence of his work. Such a sociable individuality contrasts with the self-enclosure that is implicit in the idea of "autonomy," which means giving a law to oneself. The idea of autonomy denies that we are born into a world that existed prior to us. It posits an essential alone-ness; an autonomous being is free in the sense that a being sev-ered from all others is free.[3] To regard oneself this way is to betray the natural debts we owe to the world, and commit the moral error of ingratitude. For in fact we are basically depend-ent beings: one upon another, and each on a world that is not of our making.

To live wakefully is to live in full awareness of this, our human situation. To live *well* is to reconcile ourselves to it, and try to realize whatever excellence we can. For this some eco-nomic conditions are more favorable than others. When the conception of work is removed from the scene of its execution, we are divided against one another, and each against himself. For thinking is inherently bound up with doing, and it is in rational activity together with others that we find our peculiar satisfaction.

A humane economy would be one in which the possibility of achieving such satisfaction is not foreclosed ahead of time for most people. It would require a sense of scale. We in the West have arranged our institutions to prevent the concentration of political power, with such devices as the separation of legisla-tive, executive, and judicial functions. But we have failed utterly to prevent the concentration of economic power, or take account of how such concentration damages the conditions under which full human flourishing becomes possible (it is never guaranteed). The consolation we seek in shopping serves only to narcotize us against a recognition of these facts, even while contributing to the Giant Pool of Money.

Too often, the defenders of free markets forget that what we really want is free men. Having a few around requires an economy in which the virtue of independence is cultivated, and a diversity of human types can find work to which they are suited. It is time to dispel the long-standing confusion of private property with corporate property.[4] Conservatives are right to extol the former as a pillar of liberty, but when they put such arguments in the service of the latter, they become apologists for the ever-greater concentration of capital. The result is that opportunities for self-employment and self-reliance are preempted by distant forces.

It remains for others, better versed in public policy and shrewder about its unintended consequences, to suggest ways in which the space for entrepreneurship can be protected. I would like to recommend a progressive-republican approach to the problem, which would be at once prickly and aspiring. Let us say that republicanism is a tribunal spirit that looks with active hostility on whatever erodes the stature of man. Progressivism entertains visions of a better world. A progressive-republican disposition would take its bearings from our shared potential to realize what is best in the human condition, and regard the conditions for its realization as a common weal that is not to be vandalized with impunity.

But it seems best to conclude by registering a note of sobriety, as against hopes for transformation. If cultural despair rests on a view of history as being more powerful than individuals, the revolutionary for his part entertains an exaggerated fantasy of world changing. A heady vision of the progressive hereafter in which economic antagonism has been overcome may come to stand in for, and distract him from, the smaller but harder work of living well in *this* life. The alternative to revolution, which I want to call Stoic, is resolutely this-worldly. It insists on the permanent, local viability of what is best in human beings. In practice, this means seeking out the cracks where individual agency and the love of knowledge can be realized today, in one's own life.

Acknowledgments

I'd like to thank first the tradespeople who took the time to talk with me about their work. Especially informative and helpful were Fred Cousins of Triple "O" Service, Bob Eubank of Pro Class Cycles, Jason Hosick of Marshall's Service Center, Scott Bruington at Diesel Power of Virginia, Dwayne of Spicer Automotive, Kenny of B&W Auto, Larry DeSouza of DeSouza Heating, Wendell of A&E (Appliances and Electronics), Warren of Pop-a-Lock, Stuart of Ballos Precision Machine, and the metal fabricators Charles Yeager and Chris Hildebrand. I also want to thank Tom Hull, who teaches a variety of shop programs at Marshfield High School in Coos Bay, Oregon, and Dennis Mattoon, who teaches automotive technology at Reynolds High School in Troutdale, Oregon.

This book probably wouldn't have been written if not for my relationship with Thomas Van Auken. In the years 2002–5, our efforts to figure out what was wrong with our customers' motorcycles often digressed into broader discussions of art, machines, and economics as we huddled close to a feeble propane heater, or took turns near the window fan, in a decaying warehouse in Shockoe Bottom. This book grows out of those conversations.

The craftsmen of Taylor and Boody, who build pipe organs, were extremely generous in explaining their work to me on my frequent visits. An account of their work was originally going to be part of this book but will appear instead as a separate book, to be entitled *The Organ Maker's Shop*.

The Institute for Advanced Studies in Culture at the University of Virginia has supported me in writing this book. The conversation there is unusually bold and searching, and I attribute this to the incubator environment established by James Hunter and Joe Davis. I thank them for including me. In the halls of beautiful Watson Manor, the Institute's home, I have had many conversations that pointed me down paths I wouldn't otherwise have taken. In particular, Joe Davis, Talbot Brewer, and David Franz have been the source of key insights and criticisms. They will recognize many of their own thoughts here, hopelessly enmeshed with my own. David Ciepley also helped me to see some things more clearly. Together, I take this group to be working out a new way of thinking about economics, or perhaps recovering an older way, so that it becomes once again a humanistic discipline. Others at the Institute introduced me to thinkers I now find indispensable. Josh Yates turned me on to the writings of Albert Borgmann; Andrew Witmer introduced me to Michael Polanyi; Chris Nichols gave me a book of Jackson Lears; Amy Gilbert pointed me to Iris Murdoch. Somehow I had never read Alasdair MacIntyre before he was assigned in the Institute's Friday seminar, led by Slavica Jakelic. MacIntyre's influence is evident throughout these pages. The ancient historian Xenophon reports Socrates saying, "The treasures . . . left written in books, I turn over and peruse in company with my friends, and if we find anything good in them, we pick it out, and think it a great gain if we thus become useful to one another."

I have benefited from conversations with Maria Pia Chirinos, James Poulos, Susan Arellano, Krishan Kumar, and Steve Talbot. David Novitsky gave me some very penetrating comments on chapter 3. Matthew Feeney read the entire manuscript and suggested countless improvements. What can I say about Feeney? He's the guy whose e-mails I most look forward to. We find the same things worthy of praise or blame, and together I think we have been honing the edge of a certain critical dispensation that has yet to be named. Eric Cohen and Adam Keiper, both of *The New Atlantis,* gave me an outlet for writings that wouldn't have been printed anywhere else, and helped to shape the essay that gave rise to this book. Vanessa Mobley, my editor at Penguin and an expert builder of books, brought real sympathy for the material and helped me in crucial ways to bring out its potential.

I want to thank my mother for her sensitivity to the finer things, my father for showing me that thinking is the highest pleasure, and my sister for sharing the weirdness of our childhood. Without the courage, wisdom, and endurance of my wife B., I never could have taken on the hazards of entrepreneurship, nor those of writing. An amazingly clear-headed woman, she read and critiqued drafts of every chapter. Our shared effort to understand how the mind works revealed complementary approaches, and brought our minds more closely intertwined. Finally, I thank my daughters G., aged three, and J., aged one, simply for being adorable.

Notes

I: A Brief Case for the Useful Arts

1. As reported by the Associated Press at CNN.com on October 2, 2006: "Rebuilding Shop Classes in U.S. High Schools."
2. Ibid.
3. My circumstances were a bit unusual—I lived in a large commune from age nine to fifteen. Because the group picked up and moved every six months, there was constant renovation work on whatever dilapidated hotel we currently occupied. The electrical crew needed somebody small to fit into tight crawl spaces and drafted me. I mention this only because the reader may wonder why I was working rather than attending school.
4. Alexandre Kojève, *Introduction to the Reading of Hegel: Lectures on the Phenomenology of Spirit* (Ithaca: Cornell University Press, 1989), p. 27.
5. In fact, I think residential electrical work must be the least demanding of the building arts, in terms of the skill involved. Carpenters and plumbers both have to make rigid elements fit together just right, whereas residential wiring is encased in sheathing that is flexible. Installation goes very fast. No doubt one reason for the high wages of electricians is that people are afraid of electricity, and the stakes are indeed high if it isn't done right. But getting it right isn't that hard.

So I am perfectly happy to concede the term "craft" to those who would reserve it for more demanding work, if they will allow it to include the bending of rigid conduit.

6. Hannah Arendt, *The Human Condition* (Chicago: University of Chicago Press, 1958), p. 95.

7. These features of narcissism were pointed out by Christopher Lasch in *The Culture of Narcissism* (1979).

8. In her review of Benjamin Barber's book *Consumed*, Josie Appleton writes, "It is not so much that we have an ethic of consumption, but that—by default—it remains as one of the few meaningful experiences in our lives. There is a tangibility and satisfaction to buying—to picking out a new shirt or a new album and taking it home—that means that shopping remains for individuals a confirmation of their power to make things happen in the world. The power of consumption has been usefully theorised by the Marxist sociologist Georg Simmel. In *The Philosophy of Money*, he looks at how buying an object is an act of individual subjectivity, the person stamping himself on a thing and claiming his right to its exclusive enjoyment. Simmel cited the example of a friend he knew who would buy beautiful things, not to use them, but to 'give an active expression to his liking of the things, to let them pass through his hands and, in so doing, to set the stamp of his personality upon them.' Shopping remains a way in which our choices have a tangible effect, in which we can make something in our lives new and different. It also becomes the primary way in which people can enjoy the creativity and efforts of others, even if this is done unconsciously, without knowing who made something or how" ("The Cultural Contradictions of Consumerism"; available at www.spiked-online.com/index.php?/site/reviewofbooks_article/5026).

9. *Gorgias*, 465a.

10. Mike Rose, *The Mind at Work: Valuing the Intelligence of the American Worker* (New York: Penguin Books, 2005), p. xiii.

11. Aristotle, *On Generation and Corruption*, 316a5–9.

12. Mike Eisenberg and Ann Nishioka Eisenberg, "Shop Class for the Next Millennium: Education Through Computer-Enriched Handicrafts," *Journal of Interactive Media in Education* 98 (October 14, 1998).

13. Rose, *The Mind at Work*, pp. 156-7.

14. T. J. Jackson Lears, *No Place of Grace: Antimodernism and the Transformation of American Culture, 1880-1920* (Chicago: University of Chicago Press, 1994), p. xv.

15. Ibid., p. 76.

16. Robert Franklin Hoxie, *Scientific Management and Labor* (New York and London: D. Appleton and Company, 1918), pp. 133–4.

17. Lears, *No Place of Grace*, p. 83.

18. Alan S. Blinder, "Offshoring: The Next Industrial Revolution?" *Foreign Affairs* (March/April 2006).

19. Alan S. Blinder, "Free Trade's Great, but Offshoring Rattles Me," *Washington Post,* May 6, 2007, p. B04.

20. Frank Levy, "Education and Inequality in the Creative Age," Cato Unbound, June 9, 2006, available at www.cato-unbound.org/2006/06/09/frank-levy/.

2: The Separation of Thinking from Doing

1. Harry Braverman, *Labor and Monopoly Capital: The Degradation of Work in the Twentieth Century* (New York: Monthly Review Press, 1974), p. 86.

2. Frederick Winslow Taylor, *Principles of Scientific Management* (New York and London: Harper and Brothers, 1915), p. 36.

3. Frederick Winslow Taylor, *Shop Management* (New York and London: Harper and Brothers, 1912), pp.98–9.

4. Ibid., p. 105. See the response to Taylor by N. P. Alifas, President of District No. 44, International Association of Machinists, in their

dueling testimony before the U.S. Congress, in *Industrial Relations: Final Report and Testimony,* submitted to the Congress in 1916 by the Commission on Industrial Relations, vol. 1, pp. 940 ff.

5. Braverman, *Labor and Monopoly Capital,* p. 181.

6. George Sturt, *The Wheelwright's Shop* (Cambridge: Cambridge University Press, 1993), p. 45.

7. Keith Sward, *The Legend of Henry Ford* (New York: Rinehart, 1948), p. 49.

8. Braverman, *Labor and Monopoly Capital,* p. 150.

9. Thomas A. Kinney, *The Carriage Trade: Making Horse-Drawn Vehicles in America* (Baltimore and London: The Johns Hopkins University Press, 2004), p. 241.

10. Krishan Kumar, *From Post-Industrial to Post-Modern Society: New Theories of the Contemporary World* (Cambridge, Mass.: Blackwell Publishers, 1995), p. 33.

11. T. J. Jackson Lears, "The American Way of Debt," *New York Times Magazine,* June 11, 2006.

12. Barbara Garson, *The Electronic Sweatshop: How Computers Are Transforming the Office of the Future into the Factory of the Past* (New York: Penguin, 1989), pp. 120–21.

13. Richard Florida, *The Rise of the Creative Class: And How It's Transforming Work, Leisure, Community and Everyday Life* (New York: Basic Books, 2002), pp. 6 and 8.

14. Richard Florida, "The Future of the American Workforce in the Global Creative Economy," Cato Unbound, June 4, 2006, available at www.cato-unbound.org/2006/06/04/richard-florida/.

15. Ibid.

16. Levy, "Education and Inequality in the Creative Age."

17. This is Craig Calhoun's formulation of one of Jackall's findings. Craig Calhoun, "Why Do Bad Careers Happen to Good Managers?" *Contemporary Sociology* 18, no. 4 (July 1989), p. 544.

18. Florida, *The Rise of the Creative Class,* p. 10. Barbara Ehrenreich

offers a sardonic take on such devices, which she encountered while undergoing an orientation program to work at Wal-Mart. "Sam [Walton] always said, and is shown saying, 'the best ideas come from the associates'—for example, the idea of having a 'people greeter,' an elderly employee (excuse me, associate) who welcomes each customer as he or she enters the store. Three times during the orientation, . . . we are reminded that this brainstorm originated in a mere associate, and who knows what revolutions in retailing each one of us may propose? Because our ideas are welcome, more than welcome, and we are to think of our managers not as bosses but as 'servant leaders'. . . ." *Nickel and Dimed* (New York: Metropolitan Books, 2001), p. 144.

19. Braverman, *Labor and Monopoly Capital,* p. 39.
20. Ibid., p. 444.

3: To Be Master of One's Own Stuff

1. And in fact, it must be admitted that there is something delusional about this man. The handle on the faucet might be seen as flattering the user that he has something to do with the appearance of the water, when in fact it is conveyed to his hands by a whole infrastructure of plumbing to which he pays no mind. The decisive change occurred when he no longer had to fetch water himself from the river; the disappearance of the handle perhaps brings his dependence on others to his awareness, and this is the source of his discomfort.

2. Phil Irving, "How Engines Are Lubricated: The Development of Various Popular Systems," *Motor Cycling*, March 3, 1937, p. 562.

3. If Mercedes encourages superstition, General Motors does them one better and offers a comprehensive theology. GM introduced its OnStar system in 1997, first in a few Cadillac models, and by 2004 in most GM models. Using the car's onboard diagnostics, it runs a monthly check and sends you an e-mail report. In addition to any

problems that may appear, it includes the miles remaining until your next scheduled oil change. It also lets you know if your tire pressure is low. But GM realized there was a greater opportunity, and integrated onboard systems with the cell phone and Global Positioning System infrastructure. At the OnStar Command Center, they are able to map the car's location onto a grid of 911 response jurisdictions. If the car's computer senses that the air bags have deployed, OnStar places a call to the driver. If the occupants of the car need assistance, or there is no response, OnStar informs the local emergency response services, and is able to give them the car's location. Instead of a car that needs to be taken care of, we now have a car that takes care of you.

4. There are yet other layers to the musician's obedience: she plays a prior composition. Or she may improvise, but does so within given melodic forms. These are not natural necessities, but rather cultural ones—the Mixolydian scale, or an evening raga. At another level of musicality, she plays within a genre. It may be hard bop or West Coast cool, Hindustani or Karnataka, or some synthesis of her own, but not invention *ex nihilo*. To be sure, if one inquires historically, one finds that cultural forms *are* products of human will as exercised in the past; someone had to invent the Mixolydian scale. But from the standpoint of any particular individual in the present, they are experienced as a horizon of possibility that has already been set. Indeed, contingent cultural forms have the character of necessity for most people, we non-geniuses.

5. Iris Murdoch, *The Sovereignty of Good* (London: Routledge Classics, 2001), p. 87.

6. Albert Borgmann, *Power Failure: Christianity in the Culture of Technology* (Grand Rapids, Mich.: Brazos Press, 2003), p. 31.

7. Ibid., p. 22.

8. A friend of mine bought one of these cars. He really just needed a car, and hadn't realized that walking into the dealership was like wan-

dering naïvely into a Scientology bookstore. Part of the marketing of the Scion consists of a concerted effort to generate a cult status around the car. So for a few weeks after he bought it, he'd get "tagged," meaning that he'd come back to the parked car to find a postcard stuck on the driver's window. The postcards invited him to some get-together where he could celebrate his new Scion lifestyle with other like-minded iconoclasts, a strictly grassroots affair. It seemed like he was being followed, and it started to creep him out.

9. Anaxagoras, as quoted by Aristotle, *The Parts of Animals*, 686a. The translation is my own.

10. Martin Heidegger, *Being and Time*, trans. Joan Stambaugh (Albany: SUNY Press, 1996), I.iii.15, p. 63.

11. Of course, the usual thing is not to build a teddy bear at all, but to receive one as a gift. A teddy bear is typically not a project, but something whose characteristics are simply given, and come to be cherished. Maybe the creepiest thing about Build-a-Bear is the way it mirrors the promise of reproductive genetic engineering, which may also come to offer a menu of options. It would be interesting to know how attached children become to these optimized bears, and whether generosity and acceptance get elicited by a bear understood as a project of the Self.

12. One of my customers works as an assistant to a commercial photographer. He told his boss about the shop, and she stopped by to check it out. "Perfect!" she said. I let her use the shop as a set for some photographs. She brought a male model to play the role of motorcycle mechanic. I laid out some tools, and put a really pretty bike on the lift (a 1973 Ducati 750GT). The model proceeded to hold the tools and look intently at the bike while she snapped away. I asked what the photos would be used for, and she said they would be "stock photos" that she would hope to sell to some corporate client, yet to be determined. I gather the images of work she collected were in demand for general marketing purposes.

4: The Education of a Gearhead

1. I grew up in a commune; see note 3 of chapter 1.

2. In his history of the carriage trade, Kinney tells the story of one Ezra Stratton, who began his seven-year indentured apprenticeship at a southern Connecticut carriage maker in 1824. To his disgust, sixteen-year-old Ezra found that "his first morning's work consisted of repairing the stone wall around his master's two-acre field." "In a time and place when many workshops were extensions of the master's home, the line between habitation and business was blurred at best." At lunch, young Ezra noticed "the glee of a seventeen-year-old apprentice at the table, [and] quickly divined the cause." As he would write later in his own autobiography, "the cow and horse, the pig and woodpile no longer claimed *his* attention . . . for his initiatory year of 'chores' had expired" (Kinney, *The Carriage Trade*, p. 42).

3. This is the lesson of Solon's poem according to Werner Jaeger, as quoted by David Roochnik, *Of Art and Wisdom: Plato's Understanding of Techne* (University Park: Penn State Press, 1996), p. 29.

4. As the German philosopher Friedrich Jacobi (1743–1819) characterized the central doctrine of the Kantian revolution, "we can grasp an object only insofar as we can let it come into being before us in thoughts, can make or create it in the understanding" (Jacobi as quoted by David Lachterman, *The Ethics of Geometry: A Genealogy of Modernity* [New York: Routledge, 1989], p. 9). Yet this is merely the completion of an earlier revolution. Beginning with Copernicus and Galileo, "the decision was taken to undo the habitual subordination of mind to the (pregiven) 'object' of inquiry by making the latter's intelligibility depend on what the inquirer has inserted in the object in advance, in accordance with the relevant concept he has of it" (ibid., p. 11). The procedure of the newly mathematized physics came to be taken as the model for modern thought in its entirety.

This is evident in, for example, Gassendi's dictum that "whatever we know, we know in virtue of mathematics" (ibid., p. viii).

5. Aristotle, *Rhetoric*, 1355b12.

6. Once I went with my father to see Cirque du Soleil, the famous circus. As we took our seats, he looked up at the torches burning overhead and said, "Ah, sodium yellow." When sodium burns, it gives off a yellow color, which my dad liked to explain in terms of quantum mechanics. But in fact they weren't torches; they were strips of yellow ribbon blown by a fan, with a light shining on them, to produce an artful imitation of burning torches. I pointed this out to my dad, and he was genuinely shaken by the revelation. Embarrassed for him, I suggested maybe it was his eyeglasses, but his intellectual honesty was such that he had no interest in trying to save face. He insisted that no, he could now plainly see that they were ribbons, not torches, yet he had seen torches before. The fact that he was disturbed by this experience, and open about it rather than defensive, impressed on me once more his genuine love of truth. Yet it seemed to me that the intellectual habits of his scientific training had gotten in the way of a true perception.

7. This distinction I want to make between attentiveness and assertiveness may be found in agriculture as well, corresponding to "organic" (or traditional) versus industrial methods. Industrial agriculture is assertive in the sense that it imposes its plan on the land, and reliably attains its object. It is demonstrative; the fruit it produces is the conclusion of a radically simplified ecological syllogism. The land is a kind of abstract grid upon which is projected the intention of the farmer; that intention is not much conditioned by the peculiarities of the land, because the land is treated as basically pliable. Traditional agriculture, on the other hand, regards the land as having a reality of its own. Farming in this way has the chancy, elusive character of a stochastic art, and indeed it often fails. It is subject to contingencies that do not arise from the will of the farmer, and he

must subordinate his intention to them. This was especially so in the days of animal power, but remains true to some degree of traditional agriculture as practiced today. Adam Smith wrote that "the man who ploughs the ground with a team of horses or oxen, works with instruments of which the health, strength, and temper, are very different upon different occasions. The condition of the materials which he works upon too is as variable as that of the instruments he works with, and both require to be managed with much judgment and discretion" (*The Wealth of Nations*, ed. Edwin Cannan [Chicago: University of Chicago Press, 1976], Bk. 1, Ch. X, Pt. II, p. 142). Recall George Sturt's description of similar variability in the work of the wheelwright on p. 41. Traditional agriculture is opportunistic like a conversation; paths forward open up through a dialectic between what one wants and what nature affords. For a richly descriptive account of industrial versus traditional agriculture, see Michael Pollan, *The Omnivore's Dilemma*. In his various works, Wendell Berry reflects on how agricultural practices give rise to another sort of rural ecology—a web of human relationships that may be flourishing or impoverished.

8. Murdoch, *The Sovereignty of Good*, p. 84.

9. Robert Pirsig, *Zen and the Art of Motorcycle Maintenance: An Inquiry into Values* (New York: William Morrow and Company, 1974), p. 32.

10. Ibid., pp. 32–3.

11. Ibid., pp. 33–4.

12. If it is surprising for us to learn that our word "idiot" has an origin in the idea of privacy or self-enclosure, it is surely because our thinking takes place within a horizon shaped by modern philosophy, beginning with Descartes. It was Descartes who insisted on the radically private character of rationality, thereby driving a wedge between reason and ethics.

13. Murdoch, *The Sovereignty of Good*, p. 82.

14. Ibid., p. 91.
15. Ibid., p. 88.
16. Hoxie, *Scientific Management and Labor*, p. 134.

5: The Further Education of a Gearhead

1. The wages of motorcycle mechanics are considerably lower than those of car mechanics. The economics of this are complicated, and made a bit opaque by the fact that it is a touchy matter. I have asked more experienced independent motorcycle mechanics, with shop rates of sixty, seventy, or even eighty dollars per hour (in more expensive, northern and West Coast urban markets), what percentage of time they spend in the shop is billable, and I have never gotten a straight answer.
2. Paul J. Griffiths, "The Vice of Curiosity," *Pro Ecclesia* XV/1 (2006), pp. 47–63.
3. Amy Gilbert, "Vigilance and Virtue: In Search of Practical Wisdom," *Culture* (Fall 2008), p. 8.

6: The Contradictions of the Cubicle

1. James Poulos, "Some Enchanted Bureaucracy," *Society* (May/June 2008), p. 295.
2. Linda Eve Diamond and Harriet Diamond, *Teambuilding That Gets Results: Essential Plans and Activities for Creating Effective Teams* (Naperville, Ill.: Sourcebooks, 2007), p. 108.
3. Jonathan Imber offered this perfect phrase in another context.
4. Schumpeter adds in a footnote, "At present this development is viewed by most people from the standpoint of the ideal of making educational facilities of any type available to all who can be induced to use them. This ideal is so strongly held that any doubts about it

are almost universally considered to be nothing short of indecent . . ." (*Capitalism, Socialism and Democracy* [1942; New York: Harper-Perennial, 1975], p. 152).

5. In the usage that was once most common, the word "information" denoted a report about the state of the world. It could also mean instructions for altering the world, as in a recipe for beef stew. But in the 1940s, Claude Shannon of Bell Laboratories used it in a new way. His perspective was that of a mathematician who was trying to clarify some concepts that would be helpful to electrical engineers working for the telephone company. As used by Shannon, the word is no longer tied to the semantic content of utterances as grasped by sender and receiver; "information" in the new usage refers to the transmission of meaning rather than meaning itself, and it is *quantitative*, "a measure of the difficulty in transmitting the sequences produced by some information source" (according to Warren Weaver, "The Mathematics of Communication," *Scientific American* [July 1949], p. 12, as cited by Theodore Roszak, *The Cult of Information: A Neo-Luddite Treatise on High Tech, Artificial Intelligence, and the True Art of Thinking* [Berkeley: University of California Press, 1994], p. 12). In the new usage, "even gibberish might be 'information' if somebody cared to transmit it," as Roszak writes. Shannon's appropriation of the common word "information" for this purpose has led to all manner of confusion, and infected our common use of the word in such a way that one must make an extra effort to preserve the idea of *meaning* if that is what one intends. The net effect is to embolden our native tendency to intellectual leveling, and make it seem somehow in harmony with technological progress.

6. Alexis de Tocqueville wrote,

> *Men of democratic centuries like general ideas because they exempt them from studying particular cases; they contain, if I can express myself so, many things in a small volume and give out a large*

*product in a little time. When, therefore, after an inattentive and brief examination, they believe they perceive a common relation among certain objects, they do not push their research further, and without examining in detail how these various objects resemble each other or differ, they hasten to arrange them under the same formula in order to get past them (*Democracy in America, *trans. Harvey C. Mansfield and Delba Winthrop [Chicago: University of Chicago Press, 2000], p.414).*

Trying to get past things with haste is incompatible with dwelling in things and giving them their due. But Tocqueville also suggests that the kind of attention demanded by practical involvement can serve as a corrective to this tendency. General ideas appeal to people "only in matters that are not habitual and necessary objects of their thoughts" (ibid., p. 416). Further, "those in commerce will readily seize all the general ideas one presents to them relative to philosophy, politics, the sciences, and the arts without looking at them closely; but they will entertain those that have reference to commerce only after examination and will accept them only with reservation" (ibid.). This statement requires a crucial qualification in our day. In Tocqueville's era there was no such thing as commerce without practical involvement and the kind of attention it demands, whereas in our time the separation of thinking from doing has disburdened the commercial officer class of such attention, and made it more susceptible to general ideas.

7. Among the "promising personality characteristics" listed in a current textbook of organizational psychology is "tolerance for contradiction." Frank J. Landy and Jeffrey M. Conte, *Work in the 21st Century: An Introduction to Industrial and Organizational Psychology*, 2nd ed. (Malden, Mass.: Blackwell Publishing, 2007), p. 102.

8. In fact, I think this theoretical ideal of monopoly behavior posits more omniscience than many businesses really possess. Demand-side

feedback is provided quickly in a supermarket. But when your customer is an institution, such as a library, there are unique rigidities on the demand side. How does a library solicit the expression of disgust from patrons? Instead the InfoTrac terminal simply sits unused.

9. Craig Calhoun, "Why Do Bad Careers Happen to Good Managers?" *Contemporary Sociology* 18, no. 4 (July 1989), p. 543. My account of Jackall's findings is heavily indebted to this review.

10. Robert Jackall, *Moral Mazes: The World of Corporate Managers* (New York: Oxford University Press, 1988), p. 136.

11. Ibid.

12. Ibid.

13. Ibid., p. 105.

14. Charles Murray, *Real Education* (New York: Random House, 2008), p. 103.

15. From a 2002 article in the *Chronicle of Higher Education*, as quoted by Noel Weyrich in the *Pennsylvania Gazette*, March/April 2006. It was Weyrich's article that alerted me to some of the literature I cite in this section.

16. Phillip Brown and Richard Scase, *Higher Education and Corporate Realities: Class, Culture and the Decline of Graduate Careers* (London: UCL Press, 1994), p. 138.

17. David Labaree, *How to Succeed in School Without Really Learning: The Credential Race in American Education* (New Haven, Conn.: Yale University Press, 1997), p. 3.

18. Ivar Berg, *Education and Jobs: The Great Training Robbery* (New York: Praeger Publishers, 1970).

19. Labaree, *How to Succeed*, p. 2.

20. Ibid.

21. Ibid., p. 13.

22. Where does this leave the bright kid from a lower-middle-class family who gets stellar SAT scores, studies hard, gets into a good college,

and earns good marks there while working a part-time job? That job is sure to take time away from the extracurricular socialization process where the right attitudes are instilled, the subtle cues of self-presentation are learned, and cultural capital accrues. Brown and Scase write that "unless job applicants share the same cultural understandings and disposition as the recruiter, they will find it difficult to 'decode' the rules by which the selection process is being played" (*Higher Education and Corporate Realities*, p. 22). At the same time, the student's need to send the right signals *now*, while still a student, is more desperate than ever, because with "flatter" hierarchies there is less opportunity for advancement within an organization. There isn't much of a ladder of middle management to be climbed, and positions at the top are filled by horizontal recruitment from outside the firm.

23. David A. Franz, *The Ethics of Incorporation* (Ph.D. dissertation, Sociology Department, University of Virginia, 2009), p. 71.

24. Ibid.

25. Philip Rieff, *The Triumph of the Therapeutic* (New York: Harper and Row, 1966), p. 236.

26. Diamond and Diamond, *Teambuilding That Gets Results*, pp. 110–11.

27. Ibid., pp. 58–60.

28. Ibid. p. 60.

29. I owe the formulations of this paragraph to Manuel Lopez. In a related vein, he likens eruptions of obligatory office fun to "a high school pep rally, without the more natural enthusiasms generated by cheerleaders. They're more like pep rallies led by a principal and middle-aged teachers, for example those 'say no to drugs, get high on life!' rallies that forced one to view the stoners with a new respect, or at least discover within oneself newfound powers of contempt" (personal communication).

30. See Landy and Conte, *Work in the 21st Century*, p. 169.

31. Diamond and Diamond, *Teambuilding That Gets Results*, p. 151.

32. Ibid., p. 140.

33. Ibid., p. 150.

34. I don't want to idealize the trades. One of the worst jobs I ever had was on a large crew building a Home Depot in Southern California. The electrical work was well along by the time I joined, and a couple of the other electricians made a game of sending me off on wild-goose chases to find tools and materials that didn't exist (it was only later that I realized this was what was going on). I got very little work done, and after a few days I was fired. Because there is little supervision by higher-ups on a job site, there is probably more abuse of workers by other workers in the trades than in the office. The new guy, the nonwhite guy, and the woman are especially likely to incur extra hardships.

35. Jackall, *Moral Mazes*, p. 135.

36. J. Henderlong and M. R. Lepper, "The Effects of Praise on Children's Intrinsic Motivation: A Review and Synthesis," *Psychological Bulletin* 128, no. 5 (2002), pp. 774–95, as quoted by Murray, *Real Education*, p. 130.

37. Murray, *Real Education*, p. 130.

7: Thinking as Doing

1. Anaxagoras as quoted by Aristotle, *The Parts of Animals*, 686a.

2. Heidegger, *Being and Time*, trans. Stambaugh, p. 63.

3. This is my own, somewhat free translation of *Clouds* 223–233.

4. This error can be made even by someone who handles real shoelaces every day. This illustrates the power of abstractions to falsify experience, or rather displace it.

5. Daniel Bell, *The Coming of Post-Industrial Society: A Venture in Social Forecasting* (New York: Basic Books, 1973), pp. 29–30.

6. Ibid., p. 32. In this and many other passages in the book, one isn't

sure if Bell himself adheres to the argument on offer. The passage I have quoted is in fact Bell's paraphrase of an argument by one Jay Forrester. Bell seems to distance himself from it on the next page (he calls the project of trying to rationally order society through the deployment of intellectual technology a utopian dream that has faltered), yet the whole thread of the book depends on its validity, and indeed Bell affirms it in statements published later. Kevin Robins and Frank Webster detail Bell's contradictions and suggest they are "functional"—they do important rhetorical work. See their "Information as Capital: A Critique of Daniel Bell," in Jennifer Daryl Slack and Fred Fejes, eds., *The Ideology of the Information Age* (New York: Ablex Publishing Corporation, 1987), pp. 95–117.

7. As quoted by Bruce Bower, "Seeing through Expert Eyes: Ace Decision Makers May Perceive Distinctive Worlds," *Science News* 154, no. 3 (July 18, 1988), p. 44. Klein says further that "When difficulties arise, experts find opportunities for improvising solutions."

8. See especially Michael Polanyi, *The Tacit Dimension* (Chicago: University of Chicago Press, 1966).

9. Hubert L. Dreyfus and Stuart E. Dreyfus, "From Socrates to Expert Systems: The Limits and Dangers of Calculative Rationality," available at http://socrates.berkeley.edu/~hdreyfus/html/paper_socrates.html.

10. A. D. De Groot, *Thought and Choice in Chess* (The Hague: Mouton, 1965).

11. This elegant variation on De Groot's original study, using the random condition, was conducted by W. G. Chase and H. A. Simon, "Perception in Chess," *Cognitive Psychology* 4 (1973), pp. 55–81.

12. See, above all, Michael Wheeler, *Reconstructing the Cognitive World: The Next Step* (Cambridge, Mass.: MIT Press, 2005).

13. For an excellent account, see Jean-Pierre Dupuy, *The Mechanization of the Mind: On the Origins of Cognitive Science* (Princeton: Princeton University Press, 2000).

14. It may be interesting to note that the *origins* of computer science

coincide with an insight that seems to grant the human its due. The discipline grew out of early-twentieth-century developments in logic. Gödel's theorem proves logically that some true statements, the truth of which is easily seen by human beings, cannot be *proved* to be true by the application of any formal system of rules. A computer that tries to do so will chase its tail indefinitely, never halting at an answer (the so-called halting problem). Alan Turing recognized that this meant that human minds are able to perform "uncomputable" operations. According to Andrew Hodges, Turing's 1938 Ph.D. thesis posed the question: "What is the consequence of supplementing a formal system with uncomputable deductive steps? In pursuit of this question, Turing introduced the definition of an 'oracle' which can supply on demand an answer to the halting problem for every Turing machine," that is, for every digital computer. Turing "effectively *identified* the uncomputable 'oracle' with intuition" of the sort used by mathematicians in proving theorems, and in particular "the human act of seeing the truth of a formally unprovable Gödel statement" (Andrew Hodges, "Uncomputability in the Work of Alan Turing and Roger Penrose," a lecture available at www.turing.org.uk/philosophy/lecture1.html). The essential feature of the oracle is that it performs steps which cannot be realized by any mechanical process.

During World War II, Turing participated in the Enigma codebreaking program, which used highly routinized methods. Through this experience he came to be more interested in what machines *can* do than in what they cannot. "Turing concluded that the scope of computability was *not* limited to processes where the mind follows an explicitly given rule. Machines which modified their own rules of behavior would show features which had not been foreseen by anyone designing them" (ibid., Part 2). "Turing concluded that the function of the brain was that of a machine, but one so complex that it could have the appearance of not following any rule" (ibid.). In today's computer science the hot topic is "neural networks," so called because they imitate the parallel architecture of the brain, and execute computations that can deviate from a programmer's explicit plan. They "learn" by varying the strength of connections between logical nodes, just as neural pathways get "burned" into the brain through repetition, as when one practices the piano or recites Latin noun declensions. If there is any hope for artificial intelligence, it probably lies in this direction.

15. The fragility of digitized information is like that of language; omitting the word "not" from a sentence may reverse its meaning. And of course this is no mere analogy; digitized information *is* a representation of the world by language, in a sense. But consider. The omission of the word "not" from an English sentence can usually be detected (for example, by a copy editor) because it will seem wrong *given the context*. The omission can then be discounted; natural language is robust in this way. The fragility of code is due to the fact that it is a set of instructions for a mechanical device, rather than a locus of meaning, as language is. In comprehending a word or a sentence, a human being integrates it with the larger context of a paragraph, or the pragmatics of some communicative situation (a joke, for example)—in any case, with some wider sphere of meaning. Doing so seems to be the special province of mind.

16. Maybe if you spend big money on a Fluke meter, rather than a Craftsman, you don't get this problem. I don't know. In any case it's a strange name to give to a measuring instrument, since one criterion of a true measurement is that it is repeatable. A mechanic who is paranoid could be forgiven for suspecting there is some massive joke being played out.

17. John Muir, *How to Keep Your Volkswagen Alive,* first published in 1969.

18. Thus, in working on a 2005 Suzuki GSX-R 600, you should heed the following: "When using the multi-circuit tester, do not storongly [sic] touch the terminal of the ECM coupler with a needle pointed

tester probe to prevent the terminal damage or terminal bend." I take this to mean: Be gentle with the ECM coupler; its pins are easily bent. If you should get trouble code C42, the problem is "Ignition switch signal is not input to the ECM. *When the I.D. agreement is not verified." Scanning the bottom of the page for the asterisk, we find "Immobilizer system is equipped model only," which I take to mean, only on models equipped with an immobilizer system. The first example is from page 4–34, GSX-R 600 Suzuki Service Manual, the second from page 4–31.

19. John R. Searle, "Minds, Brains, and Programs," *Behavioral and Brain Sciences* 3, no. 3 (September 1980).

20. In modern motorcycle manuals, you often come across a little emblem next to the description of some repair procedure, accompanied by the words "use special tool number xx–xxx." Often as not these tools can be improvised, once you know what the tool *is*. So if you work at an independent shop you try to figure out what the tool might actually be by considering the task before you, and what needs to happen. It's a matter of reverse-engineering the tool, from function to form. This is another instance where you have to peer through the obscurities in the manual and refer them to the facts before you. At a dealership you would just go to the service manager and ask for tool number xx–xxx.

8: Work, Leisure, and Full Engagement

1. In Bill Penington, "Perfection Is Afterthought, Some Perfect Examples Say," *New York Times*, Sunday, February 3, 2008, front page and p. 20.

2. Talbot Brewer, personal communication.

3. Simone Polillo, *Structuring Financial Elites: Conservative Banking and the Local Sources of Reputation in Italy and the United States, 1850–*

1914 (Ph.D. dissertation, Sociology Department, University of Pennsylvania, 2008), p. 157. As J. P. Morgan put it in the congressional hearings known as the "Money Trust" investigation of 1913, "The first thing is character. . . . [A] man I do not trust could not get the money from me on all the bonds in Christendom" (quoted by Polillo, p. 158).

4. Lamont as quoted by Polillo, *Structuring Financial Elites*, p. 159.

5. If you have ever had a friend sell your car for you, you know how this works. It's best not to burden your friend with all the details of what's wrong with the car. That way, when the buyer asks what problems the car might have, your friend can honestly say he doesn't know. This is how the used-car industry works; when you trade your car in, it is never sold to its next owner by the same dealer. Instead it passes through one or more auctions. The ownership history is purposefully obscured, the service history purposefully discarded. This keeps everyone involved morally pure. Economists speak of "asymmetric information," in which one party to a transaction has an advantage over the other, but I have seen no discussion of this phenomenon, where an entire market is predicated on the *discarding* of information. The securitizing of sketchy mortgages, and the invention of complex derivatives based on them, seems to accomplish a similar purpose (granting that it serves other purposes as well), though in this case the process is overlaid with an apparatus of mathematical complexity that spares its participants the kind of self-awareness used-car salesmen suffer. Only the person who originally writes the mortgage has to deal with that.

6. See the account of the sub-prime mortgage crisis that aired on the NPR show *This American Life:* Episode 355, "The Giant Pool of Money," available at www.thislife.org/radio_episode.aspx?episode=355.

7. I quote from pp. 11–13 of a draft manuscript of Talbot Brewer, *The*

Retrieval of Ethics, forthcoming from Oxford University Press in 2009.

8. M. P. Lepper, D. Greene, and R. E. Nisbett, "Undermining Children's Intrinsic Interest with Extrinsic Reward: A Test of the 'Overjustification' Hypothesis," *JPSP* 28 (1973), pp. 129–37.

9. The old Protestant value of devotion to work for the sake of work may instill virtues like diligence, but is mute when it comes to assessing particular kinds of work against one another. The liberal ideal of work that is *freely chosen* (as exemplified by the later writings of Betty Friedan) is similarly indiscriminate, demurring from judgments of better and worse (this resemblance was noticed by Russel Muirhead in his excellent book *Just Work*). Both of these attempts to give work transcendent meaning are in deep harmony with the market logic of fungibility, which posits an essential equivalence between all commodities. They collapse the distinctions that matter to us, and on that count would seem to misrepresent the human dimension of our productive labor. For how could the *character* of what is produced, and its meaning within the larger web of human practices in which the product is used, not cast its light of a particular hue over the activity of making, or fixing? This is especially so when the maker's or fixer's activity is enlivened by a direct perception of the thing made or fixed, being used in its full context.

10. I am also connected to other mechanics, who may judge my work in ways a rider wouldn't. Through the winter and spring of my last year in Chicago, Fred Cousins had seen only disconnected parts (the starter motor; the engine case halves) of the café racer I was building. When one day in late May I came by the shop on the finished bike, he looked it over for a few minutes without saying a word. Finally, crouching down, he pointed out that the clip holding on the master link of the drive chain was positioned 180 degrees from the traditional convention. Only later did I come to see why the conventional way is better.

11. This was brought home to me at the vintage races at Virginia International Raceway. In amateur motorcycle racing, most of the riders are their own mechanics, and they are constantly experimenting to find a competitive edge. Some are tight-lipped about their discoveries, others open. As Tommy and I wandered through the paddocks, we came across Eric Cooke, who at that time had recently held the number-one ranking in a certain class on his Honda CB350, and happened to live in Richmond. He was very generous with his track-won wisdom. The word among Richmond mechanics was that Eric, working with the Jedi knight of CB350 cylinder head gurus (whose name nobody seemed to know), had built a motor that dynoed at fifty horsepower, which is about twice the stock figure. As we talked, his race was called. Going to bump-start the bike, he found that the breather canister (actually, an empty plastic water bottle) had come loose from the frame. He was all suited, helmeted, and gloved up, so more or less helpless in this moment of panic. In an impressive display of quick thinking and decisive action, Tommy grabbed a nearby can of safety wire and a pair of pliers, and quickly wired the breather to the frame; Eric made the start.

Concluding Remarks on Solidarity and Self-Reliance

1. Murray, *Real Education*, p. 132.
2. I owe this insight to Joseph E. Davis (personal communication).
3. I owe this formulation about the lonely character of autonomy to a lecture on Dante's *Inferno* given by Anthony Esolen at the University of Virginia on November 5, 2008.
4. This error is facilitated by the legal principle of corporate "personhood." The principle was established in the 1880s, in the case of *Santa Clara County v. Southern Pacific Railroad Company*, 118 U.S. 398 (1186), where corporations were proclaimed to be "legal per-

sons" entitled to full protection of the Fourteenth Amendment. As a result, much progressive economic legislation was ruled unconstitutional because it violated an "individual's" (that is, corporation's) liberty of contract. I would like to thank Richard Brake for this history.

Index

Index

Berg, Ivar, 145
Berry, Wendell, 224 n.7
Best Buy, 48–49
Betty Crocker, 67
birds, 193
Blinder, Alan, 33–34, 164–65, 169
blue-collar work, 3, 6, 31
  degradation of, 38–44
Borgmann, Albert, 65–66
Bower, Bruce, 231 n.7
Brake, Richard, 237 n.4
Braverman, Harry, 38, 40, 42, 50
Brewer, Talbot, 186–87, 194
Brown, Phillip, 144, 147
Buggy House, 184, 186
Build-a-Bear, 69, 70, 221 n.11

Calhoun, Craig, 139
capitalism, 19, 32, 52
carpenters, 21–22, 52–53, 156, 207
centralization of thinking, 44–47, 49
Chase, W. G., 231 n.11
chess, 169–70, 171
chimpanzees, 193
choice, 50, 63, 70, 205, 206
circumspection, 123–25
Clouds (Aristophanes), 162–63
Coetzee, J. M., 104
college, 9, 19, 32, 44, 53, 129–30,
    143–48, 159
  community, 12
  and empty credentialism, 144–47
  and its signaling function, 147–48
  as training for the office, 147
Collins, Randall, 143, 147
Comaneci, Nadia, 180, 194
Coming of Post-Industrial Society, The
    (Bell), 167–68
Committee on Social Thought, 104,
    108, 111
common wealth, 188, 209
commune, author's childhood in, 74,
    75, 76, 215 n.3,
community, 27, 185–92, 198–99
  and responsibility, 189–92

of use and of making/fixing,
    185–87, 189, 196–97
community colleges, 12
compensation, wages as, 5, 43
computerized diagnostics, 35, 172–75,
    177–79
computers, 11, 23–24, 35
  human minds compared with,
    170–71
  interfaces of, 60–61
construction work, 3
consumers, 2, 7, 18, 56, 63, 70–71,
    205
  craftsmanship and, 17–18, 29
  debt of, 43–44
consumption engineers, 43
Conte, Jeffrey M., 227 n.7
Cooke, Eric, 237 n.11
Copernicus, 222 n.4
corporate culture, 148–49, 153
corporate personhood, 237 n.4
corporations, 126, 155
Cousins, Fred, 25, 106–8, 109, 116,
    207, 236 n.10
Cox, Kyle, 12–13
craftsmanship, 5–6, 13, 15, 20
  Arts and Crafts movement and,
    28–30
  consumerism and, 17–18, 29
  standards of, 18–19
creative economy, 47–52, 144
creativity, 50, 51, 53, 68, 82
crews *v.* teams, 155, 157, 160, 199
cubicle life, 126
Culture of the New Capitalism, The
    (Sennett), 17, 18, 19–20, 46–47
curiosity *v.* circumspection, 123–24

Darwinism, 193
Davis, Joseph E., 237 n.2
debt, 43–44
Deep Blue, 169, 170
degradation of work, 37
  in blue-collar jobs, 38–44
  in white-collar jobs, 44–47

240

Index

Index

Index

Index

Index